VALLETTA
City of the Knights

OLIVER GATT

'*Dum spiramus tuebimur*'

While we breathe, we shall defend

Latin Maxim

Published by Book Distributors (BDL) Limited,
13, Giorgio Preca Street,
San Gwann SGN09,
Malta.

© Oliver Gatt 2008

First published 2008

Author:	Oliver Gatt
	oliver_gatt@yahoo.com
Photography:	Oliver Gatt
Design and Layout:	Salesian Press, Malta
Graphic Designers:	Matthew Borg & Michael Conti
Printing:	Gutenberg Press, Malta
Distribution:	Book Distributors (BDL) Ltd., Malta
	www.bdlbooks.com
	info@bdlmalta.com
Illustrations:	Stephen C. Spiteri
ISBN:	978-99957-20-05-6

To the memory of John Mary Bugeja

And to my dear nephew,
Max.

FOREWORD

THE GREAT CITY
OF THE KNIGHTS

Valletta is the triumphal commitment and evidence that Malta, the southernmost castle of Christendom in Europe, has held and is victorious. Its great fortifications, its impregnability, are a promise that it will not ever lose its identity. After the Great Siege of 1565 in which the Hospitaller knights of St John battled with the Turkish armada, the bells of Europe chanted with joy, delight, and relief from nearby Syracuse all the way to Canterbury and from Lisbon across to Budapest.

The victory of the knights was accompanied by great loss of life shared with the people of Malta who were staunch and sturdy and loyal to their faith. The decision to build a new city, Valletta, to be named after the valorous Grand Master Jean Parisot de Valette became a reality backed by the generous bounty of Pope Pius V and the princes of Europe in whose interest the strength, potency, and muscle of Malta would be a main concern. The foundation stone of the new city was laid with due pomp and ceremony in 1566. The city is today surrounded by some of the finest fortifications in the world; it is the oldest surviving completely planned city of Europe and it contains some of the finest art treasures belonging to our culture and civilization.

Nicholas de Piro

Opposite: The coffered ceiling of St Anne's chapel, Fort St Elmo.

CONTENTS

Opposite: Detail from the main entrance of the Jesuit church and oratory.

The City of the Knights

INTRODUCTION

Valletta, the capital of Malta, is a UNESCO World Heritage Site. It represents a masterpiece of human creative genius inextricably linked to the history of the aristocratic Order of St John of Jerusalem which ruled over the island for almost 300 years. The city lies on a tongue of land projecting between the fine anchorages of Marsamxett and Grand Harbour. Marsamxett Harbour lies to the north of the city and is characterized by the impressive Fort Manoel and the seaside city of Sliema, Malta's premier tourist resort. To the south, the magnificent Grand Harbour is graced by the historic three cities of Birgu, Senglea, and Bormla and by the impressive forts of St Angelo and Ricasoli. The arms of the breakwater stretching across the port's mouth make this an all-weather harbour. Its many inlets and creeks have enticed many a great maritime power throughout history and have consequently shaped the history of Malta. The land on which Valletta is built rises from the waters to 52 metres. Valletta lies 345 km north-east from Tripoli (Libya) and 188 km south of Catania (Sicily). Its population is approximately 6,500 residents. The official designation of the city is *Humilissima Civitas Valletta* but it is locally referred to simply as *il-Belt*, 'the city'. Valletta's 320 monuments, all within an area of 0.55km², make it one of the most concentrated historical areas in the world.

Opposite: Republic Street at dusk.
Top: View of Valletta from Senglea.
Middle: Sunrise over Fort St Angelo, Grand Harbour.
Bottom: Fort Manoel, Marsamxett Harbour.

A BRIEF HISTORY

Early Beginnings

Before the arrival of the knights in 1530, this promontory known as Mount Sciberras (meaning 'light-point') was a sterile land, save for a few fields, and sparsely inhabited by a handful of fishermen or farmers. At the headland there stood an old chapel dedicated to St Elmo and a watchtower built in 1488 to guard the entrances of the two harbours.

In 1552, Grand Master Juan d'Homedes commissioned the architect Pietro Prado to design the star-shaped St Elmo fort on the site of the watchtower. The fort would play a key role during the Great Siege of 1565, claiming the lives of 8,000 Turkish men before falling after a bitter 30 days of constant bombardment. The knights, recognizing the strategic importance of Mount Sciberras, had been long considering erecting a fortress-city on

Above: Graphic reconstruction of Fort St Elmo.

Below: The assault on Fort St Elmo, 1565 (Detail from Grand Master's Palace fresco by Matteo Perez D'Aleccio).

this land but lack of funds and the constant fear of a Turkish assault kept the project shelved indefinitely. The Great Siege reduced the island's defences to rubble and exhausted the Order's treasury. Grand Master de Valette and the knights, fearing a renewed Ottoman attack, faced a dilemma: abandon Malta and seek refuge elsewhere or make the island their permanent home.

Left: Grand Master La Valette.
Middle: Pope Pius V.
Right: King Philip II of Spain.

A New City

De Valette rekindled the idea of a fortress-city on Mount Sciberras. He pleaded to the Christian courts of Europe for financial help to build the new city that was to serve as the shield of all Christendom. The Great Siege had elevated the Hospitallers to legendary status and monetary rewards soon began pouring in from the European courts.

King Charles IX of France donated 140,000 French *livres* and King Sebastian of Portugal sent 30,000 *cruzados*. Pope Pius V donated 35,000 *scudi* and offered the services of his military engineer Francesco Laparelli. King Philip II of Spain also sent his engineer Gabrio Serbelloni to assist in this ambitious project, together with a generous 90,000 *livres*. The European powers were only too happy to let the knights fight the infidel away from their own homes.

On 28 March 1566 the dignitaries of the Order crossed the harbour from their convent in Birgu to lay the foundation stone of the new city. The first stone was carved with the eight-pointed cross of the Hospitallers and had a cavity filled with coins and medals commemorating the events. The new city was to be called Valletta after its founder. The symbolic golden lion on a red shield, taken from de Valette's coat of arms, was chosen for the city's own coat of arms.

Under the direction of Laparelli, some 6,000 men worked everyday, day and night, in winter and summer to erect the city's fortifications before the Turks launched a new campaign against Malta. Unfortunately, de Valette did not live to see his beloved city completed. He died in the summer of 1568 and his body was interred in the chapel of St Anne (Birgu) and later in Our Lady of Victories church, making him the first person to be buried in the new city. He was succeeded by Grand Master del Monte who transferred the convent from Birgu to Valletta in March 1571.

Above: The coat of arms of the city of Valletta.
Below: Francesco Laparelli, the pope's military engineer entrusted with the planning of Valletta.
Opposite: Three dimensional reconstruction of Valletta c.1600.

An Ideal Renaissance City

Laparelli's assistant, the Maltese Gerolamo Cassar, took over the task of erecting the first buildings within the fort. The knights' residences, the Grand Master's Palace, the hospital, the foundry, the bakeries, the gunpowder factory, the windmills, and the new houses and palaces started springing up. Eight longitudinal and 12 latitudinal principal roads ran parallel to each other to allow easy artillery movement in the case of a siege. The houses had to have a well and had to be connected to the city's drainage system. The land front was protected by a series of bastions and counterguards, surmounted by the cavaliers of St James and St John. The building material was obtained from the cutting of the deep dry ditch that divides the walls from the mainland and from a proposed galley-pen on the Marsamxett side. The entrance to the harbour was defended by the repaired fort of St Elmo and the city was defended by a 320 km perimeter of

'Round this busy blue water rises rocks,
blazing in sunshine and covered with every
imaginable device of fortification.'

William M. Thackeray, 1844

Graphic view of the impregnable Valletta land front fortifications.

impregnable fortifications that fell just short of the water's edge. Grand Master Aloph de Wignacourt paid out of his own pocket for the construction of an aqueduct to carry water from the springs of Dingli and Rabat to the wells of Valletta. On 21 April 1615 water flowed from the open fountains of the capital to much rejoicing.

The increased sense of security allowed the city to flourish and the knights adorned its many palaces and churches with the finest artistic treasures. In the late 18th century, the French poet and scholar Jacques Delille wrote that the knights had accumulated enormous wealth and had turned Valletta into their private harem. Allured by trade and by the sumptuous lifestyle of their aristocratic overlords, many Maltese moved within the walls of Valletta. At the time of Delille's description, Valletta's population numbered some 20,000 inhabitants.

French Occupation

On 9 June 1798, Napoleon Bonaparte stopped at Malta on his way to Egypt. On being refused entry into Grand Harbour, he landed his 50,000 troops ashore and took the island by force. France, for so long the protector of the Order before the revolution, had provided the Hospitallers with its greatest source of fighting men and revenue. Now, German Grand Master Hompesch with his 600 knights, a third of whom were French, was at the mercy of the Corsican general. Three days later, he capitulated and Malta became a possession of the French Republic, marking the end of 268 years of Hospitaller rule.

To sustain its troops, the French army depended heavily on looting its conquered lands; soon enough, Napoleon's men under General Vaubois began robbing the island's churches of their gold and silver treasures. In less than 3 months of French rule, the Maltese revolted and the French were forced to withdraw to the safety of Valletta and the harbour fortifications. Lord Nelson, then using Sicily as a base, dispatched a naval squadron to Malta. The Maltese insurgents together with the British naval blockade at sea under Capt. Alexander Ball forced the French to surrender on 5 September 1800.

Napoleon Bonaparte crossing the Alps.

The French landing at Malta, 9 June 1798.

A British Colony

The Maltese request for the British crown to act as protector of the islands eventually led to Malta officially becoming a colony of the British Empire with the Treaty of Paris in 1814. Half-way between Gibraltar and Alexandria, Malta became a valuable asset as a naval base for the British Mediterranean fleet. The harbour area burgeoned and Valletta once again became the centre of commercial activity. The British royal arms now stood proudly inside the Grand Master's (then Governor's) Palace, the National Library, and above the Main Guard Portico. The gateways of the knights were given English

The British arms above the Main Guard in Palace Square.

names, such as Kingsgate for Porta San Giorgio and Victoria Gate for Porta del Monte. The same fate befell the street names: Strada San Giacomo became Merchants Street, Strada San Sebastiano became Old Mint Street, and Strada San Giorgio (today's Republic Street) became known as Kingsway. Inside the capital, the British left their legacy in stone with buildings such as the Royal Opera House (destroyed in 1942), St Paul's Anglican pro cathedral, and the Valletta Market. Benjamin Disraeli once declared that 'Valletta equals in its noble architecture, if even it does not excel, any capital in Europe.' The statue of Queen Victoria in Republic Square, the monument to Sir Alexander Ball in the Lower Barrakka Gardens, and the commemorative sarcophagus to Governor Sir Thomas Maitland in the Upper Barrakka Gardens are all reminders of the British era.

World War I

During the World War I, Malta reaffirmed its ancient role of caring for the sick and injured. The Holy Infirmary (and other Hospitals around the island) opened their doors to admit the wounded British, French, Australian, and New Zealand troops returning from the disastrous Gallipoli campaign. Between 1915 and 1917 some 60,000 patients were treated here, earning Malta the title of 'Nurse of the Mediterranean'. Around 2,000 war victims were buried in Malta.

The *Sette Giugno* (7 June) Riots

On 7 June 1919 the Maltese, dissatisfied with British rule in the post-war recession, gathered in Valletta in support of a National Assembly that was to draft a new self-governing constitution for Malta. British troops called in to control the escalating tension fired on the crowds. Riots broke out in the capital and four Maltese men lost their lives. The event is hailed as a landmark in the genesis of Maltese statehood. The monument commemorating the victims of the *Sette Giugno* riots is to be found in Palace Square.

Top: Sir Alexander Ball.
Middle: Holy Infirmary (Station Hospital) during World War I.
Bottom: Sette Giugno monument in Palace Square.

World War II

The Second World War came to Malta on 11 June 1940. Having declared war on Britain and France the night before, Mussolini's *Regia Aeronautica* dropped the first bombs on the island at 6.55 a.m. The first victims were four gunners at Fort St Elmo. During the initial six months of hostilities, the Italian bombing were relatively mild and did little to demoralize the local population. However, the dive-bombing attacks of the German *Luftwaffe* in early 1941 turned Valletta and the Harbour area into a blazing inferno. This was a foretaste of the fighting intensity that was to ensue in the following two years.

Field Marshal Kesserling was determined to 'wipe Malta off the map'. Bombs fell indiscriminately on the capital. The streets became impassable with rubble from the destroyed cinemas, theatres, churches, palaces, and cafes. The art treasures had

Top: The Upper Barrakka in ruins.
Above: Old Bakery Street after the blitz.

9

The Royal Opera House devastated by bombing raids, 7 April 1942.

The Triton Fountain outside City Gate.

The first president of the Republic of Malta addressing the crowds from the Palace balcony, 13 December 1974.

been removed to secure shelters, while the various government departments where transferred to safer towns in the centre of the island. The auberges of France and Auvergne, the knights' bakeries and prison and the Royal Opera House perished in the blitz. Miraculously, St John's cathedral and the Grand Master's Palace narrowly escaped total annihilation despite being hit. Most of the residents of the war ravaged cities of Valletta, Birgu, Isla, and Bormla settled down in other parts of the island, never to return. On 15 April 1942, King George VI awarded Malta the George Cross for its brave resistance in the face of overwhelming adversity.

On 2 February 1945 American President Franklin D. Roosevelt and British Prime Minister Sir Winston Churchill held a meeting, supposedly in a well beneath the Grand Master's Palace, before heading for the Big Three Conference in Yalta with Russian dictator Josef Stalin.

Post-war Reconstruction

After the war, reconstruction in Valletta began in earnest. Slum areas were replaced with new housing solutions. Kingsgate and its interior were transformed into the modernist City Gate and Freedom Square respectively. The destroyed buildings in front of St John's co cathedral gave way to a new square (St John's Square) and the Carmelite church dome changed the Valletta skyline. A new ring road was built around the city and the Triton Fountain now greeted visitors entering Valletta.

Today

In the post-war years, Malta pushed for a more representative government. On 21 September 1964 Malta acquired Independence from Britain and was declared a Republic on 13 December 1974. The last British warships left the Grand Harbour on 1 April 1979. Marble plaques commemorating these events are affixed to the façade of the Grand Master's Palace.

The palace houses the office of the president of Malta while the Auberge de Castille is the office of the prime minister. The House of Representatives is also located inside the palace, above the Armoury Museum. In 2004 Malta joined the European Union and on 1 January 2008 adopted the Euro as its currency. The reverse of the €1 and €2 coins bear the eight-pointed cross of the Hospitallers.

The House of Representatives; formerly the armoury of the Grand Master's Palace.

The Langues and their Auberges

The Order of St John was comprised of a total of eight langues or nationalities. In order of seniority, these were: Provence, Auvergne, France, Italy, Aragon, England, and Germany. Aragon was later divided to form the eighth langue of Castille (together with Portugal and Leon). To preserve their national identity, each langue built, at its own expense, its residential quarter known as an 'auberge'. In Rhodes and in Birgu, the knights resided in the *collachio*, that is an area that reserved for the brethren, their church, hospital, and auberges. In Valletta the *collachio* ideal was not adopted.

The reverse of the Maltese Euro coin.

Gerolamo Cassar built seven auberges in Valletta between 1571 and 1575. By then the langue of England had ceased to exist and the Anglo-Bavarian langue formed in 1784 eventually took up residence in Carneiro Palace, close to Fort St Elmo. Every auberge was built around a central courtyard and its façade abutted a square. These inns of residence welcomed travelling pilgrims and foreign dignitaries in search of hospitality. Every auberge had its bakery, stable, slaughter-house, tavern, and dining room. The knights ate together at fixed hours and assembled here to discuss important matters. The flags of the Order, the langue, and of the ruling grand master fluttered from the masts on top of the auberges. Of the seven auberges in Valletta, only four survive. The auberge of Auvergne in Republic Street and the auberge of France in South Street both fell victim to German bombing during the last war, while the auberge of Germany was demolished in 1839 to erect the Protestant cathedral of St Paul in its stead.

The well inside the courtyard of the Auberge d'Italie.

England

Germany

Provence

Castille

Italy

Auvergne

France

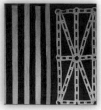

Aragon

Administration

The head of each langue was called the pilier. Depending on his provenance, the pilier was responsible for a post within the Order's governing structure. The head of the langue of Provence was the grand preceptor in charge of the treasury. The pilier of Auvergne was the marshal responsible for military administration. The post of hospitaller, entrusted with the running of the hospital, was assigned to the head of the French langue and the admiral of the Order's navy was the position held by the Italian pilier. Supplies were administered by the head of the Aragonese langue, entitled grand conservator, while the fortified outposts of the Religion, such as the coastal towers, were under the command of the German grand bailiff. The head of the langue of Castile, Leon, and Portugal was the chancellor, while that of the English langue, the turcopilier, was traditionally in charge of the cavalry. Each langue was responsible for a section of fortifications to defend in time of war and a church to adorn with artistic treasures worthy of the elite of European nobility.

The Grand Masters of the Sovereign Order of St John, Jerusalem, Rhodes, and Malta

Early in the eleventh century, some pious merchants from Amalfi founded a hospital in Jerusalem, close to the church of the Holy Sepulchre, to care for pilgrims travelling in the Holy Land. This body of men formed themselves into a brotherhood with aim of protecting and caring for the poor, the sick, and the suffering, and later came to be known as the 'Knights Hospitaller'. Brother Gerard Tum, a compassionate man of great valour and wisdom was elected head, or rector, of this fraternity in 1099. That year, Godfrey de Bouillon with the army of the First Crusade captured Jerusalem.

The fame of the Knights hospitallers and their services grew rapidly and the Order soon received generous monetary and land donations from European nobles. They opened new hospitals in the Middle East and by the mid-twelfth century they formed themselves into an Order of Military Monks with the purpose of protecting the pilgrims journeying to and from the Holy Land. In 1125, the French Raymond Du Puy was elected rector and he assumed the title of 'Master' of the Order of St John. He divided the brethren into classes: military knights, knights of honour, knights of magistral grace, chaplains, and serving brothers. As its uniform, the Order adopted the black cowl with the eight-pointed cross symbolizing the eight beatitudes. To be admitted into the Order, a candidate had to produce proofs of nobility from both sides of the family of eight quarterings.

The crusader defence at the siege of Acre against the Saracens.

When Saladin took over Jerusalem in 1187, the Order of the Knights Hospitallers found refuge in Acre, and then in Limassol (1291) until, in 1309, they attacked and conquered the island of Rhodes. The first grand master in Rhodes was Frà Foulques de Villaret and 18 grand masters succeeded him in the next 212 years on that island. The last grand master to reign in Rhodes was Frà Philippe de Villiers de L'Isle Adam. Withstanding six months of siege by the Ottoman forces of Suleiman the Magnificent, ammunitions and supplies were eventually exhausted. Seeing that no aid from European monarchs was forthcoming, L'Isle Adam and his brave knights finally surrendered. They were permitted to leave Rhodes unmolested. After seven years of roaming Europe, Emperor Charles V of Spain offered the Order the islands of Malta. After initial reluctance, L'Isle Adam finally accepted and on 26 October 1530 he entered Grand Harbour on board the carrack St Anne to claim the Order's new home.

The Ottoman Sultan, Suleiman the Magnificent.

The grand master was now subject to both emperor and pope. Still, the grand master was no less sovereign than other crowned heads of Europe. He was a true prince, often at the centre of diplomatic relations with other European monarchs. Headed by her own 'princes', Malta's importance grew in international circles. Her fleet was a force to be reckoned with, her cities and bastions envied, and the chivalric Order of the knights held in high esteem.

Twenty-eight grand masters served in Malta before Ferdinand Von Hompesch surrendered the islands to General Napoleon Bonaparte in June 1798. Of these, 11 were French, 10 Spanish, 3 Italian, 3 Portuguese, and 1 German.

Grand Master Manoel Pinto de Fonseca.

Republic Street

Eagle Street

Zachary Street

East Street

Old Mint Street

Merchants Street

Old Theatre Street

St Lucia Street

ZONE 1

1 City Gate
2 Royal Opera House
3 St Barbara Church
4 St Catherine of Italy Church
5 Our Lady of Victory Church
6 Auberge de Castille
7 St James Cavalier
8 Lascaris War Rooms
9 Garrison Chapel
10 Upper Barrakka Gardens
11 Notre Dame de Liesse Church
12 Auberge d'Italie
13 Castellania Palace
14 Palazzo Parisio
15 St James' Church

Left: The imposing Auberge of Castille rebuilt by Grand Master Pinto.

City Gate

In 1632 Grand Master De Paule commissioned the Maltese architect Tommaso Dingli to design a new baroque gate for Valletta. The gate known as Porta San Giorgio (St George's Gate) had a single carriageway flanked by two pedestrian entrances. It was a monumental two-tiered gate with rusticated features giving it a robust appearance and was crowned by four obelisk finials signifying eternity.

The bridge spans a dry moat and in the past it fell short a couple of feet away from where the drawbridge would be lowered, extending the final gap to provide access into the city. Three such gates were constructed in Valletta: Porta San Giorgio (now City Gate), Del Monte Gate (now Victoria Gate), and Marsamxett Gate (now replaced by a tunnel).

In 1853 Porta San Giorgio was rebuilt with a dual carriageway entrance. Renamed Porta Reale or Kingsgate, it kept its former robust charm but allowed better traffic flow to and from

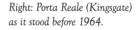

Right: Porta Reale (Kingsgate) as it stood before 1964.

18

Valletta. Two large statues representing Grand Masters L'Isle Adam (the first grand master in Malta) and de Valette (the founder of the city) were placed inside two niches above the pedestrian entrances. The bust of Pope Pius V, benefactor of the new city, was placed above the interior of Porta Reale while a plaque recalling the foundation of Valletta was affixed below the British Arms on the façade.

In 1964 the present gate replaced the old Porta Reale. The gate is still referred to by the Maltese as *Putirjal*, a corruption of 'Porta Reale', but the sentiments towards the modernist gate are very different. The new gate is alien to the architectural fabric of the baroque city and not many tears will be shed if it had to be replaced.

Above: City Gate today.
Below: The Royal Opera House in all its splendour.
Bottom: Handbill for a Royal Opera House performance, 1930.

Royal Opera House

The design of the Opera House was entrusted to Edward Middleton Barry whose portfolio included Charing Cross Hotel, the 'Barry Rooms' at the National Gallery, and Covent Garden Theatre in London.

The Theatre Royal took four years to construct, being inaugurated on 9 October 1866 to a packed house with Vincenzo Bellini's *I Puritani*. The edifice which was often in the eye of public controversy and had cost more than half the island's total revenue soon became Malta's sweetheart.

Barry's theatre was a neo-classical gem. Its heavy Corinthian-colonnaded façade receded from the main street (formerly Kingsway) upon a rusticated podium. This podium or terrace was a counter-measure for the site's 3-metre slope from Victory Square at the rear to Strada Reale (Kingsway) at the front. Coffee shops nested beneath the theatre's grand staircase and gas-lit lanterns.

The opera house had a 1,100 seated and 200 standing capacity. The season's opening in October became a national event. On

25 May 1873 fire entirely gutted the interior but left exterior intact. Four years later, on 11 October 1877, it was re-opened with Verdi's *Aida*.

Recitals, balls, farces, ballets, charity events, operas, and concerts still entertained the British, Maltese, and foreign visitors alike until the fateful night of 7 April 1942 when a German air raid attack destroyed the theatre. More than 65 years after its destruction, the former 'dream' theatre remains an embarrassing ruin. Various plans and efforts to rebuild Malta's 'sweetheart' have come to nothing. The capital still lacks its heart. The surviving 19th century podium is just a reminder of a bygone era of carriages, gas-light, hats, and royal visits.

Above: Raiders passed; the Royal Opera House in ruins.
Below: The church of the Provencal knights dedicated to St Barbara.

St Barbara Church

The church dedicated to St Barbara in Republic Street belonged to the knights of the langue of Provence. In 1737, an earlier, more modest church was demolished to make way for a newer edifice by Romano Carapecchia, who died a year later from a severe heart attack before the temple was completed.

Although other architects saw to the completion of the project, the interior was never truly finished. The painting above the main altar is the work of French artist Antoine Favray, court painter to Grand Masters Pinto and de Rohan. Painted in 1747, the scene depicts St Barbara's miraculous ascension to heaven after her martyrdom at the hands of her own father, Dioscurus.

St Barbara is the patron saint of the Confraternity of Gunners and, for a period, the church served as the seat of the Guild of Bombardiers. A three-metre gilt statue representing the Immaculate Conception adorns the façade.

St Catherine of Italy Church

Adjoining the Auberge d'Italie, St Catherine church was under the patronage of the Italian langue. Both the church and the Italian auberge suffered from the earthquake which hit Malta in 1693. In 1713, Romano Carapecchia remodelled Gerolamo Cassar's original 16th-century building, adding the elegant baroque portico. This was an innovative concept if one takes into account the strict regulations that prohibited the projections of buildings into the parallel streets of Valletta to facilitate the flow of artillery traffic in time of war. The altarpiece by Mattia Preti depicts *The Martyrdom of St Catherine*, patron saint of the Italian knights.

Our Lady of Victory Church

Dedicated to the victory of the Great Siege of 1565, this church was the first of the 25 churches to be built in Valletta and is attributed to Gerolamo Cassar. Our Lady of Victory church was the first conventual church of the new city. Construction began in 1567, just one year after laying the foundation stone of Valletta.

The church is the sum of alterations carried out in 1690 and 1752 when the lateral bell tower was added and the building embraced the new baroque ideal. The bust of Pope Innocent XI in the façade was commissioned by Grand Master Perellos in the late 17th century.

Grand Master Jean Parisot de Valette, hero of the Great Siege and founder of the city which bears his name, died on 21 August 1568. His corpse was laid to rest in this church until it was later moved to the grand masters' crypt in St John's.

Top: The church of the Italian knights dedicated to St Catherine.
Middle: Our Lady of Victory; the first church to be built in Valletta.
Bottom: Interior of the church of Our Lady of Victory.

The Auberge of Castille; nowadays the office of the prime minister.

Auberge de Castille

The first auberge on this site was a single-storey building designed by Gerolamo Cassar. In 1741 Grand Master Pinto commissioned a larger two-storey palace to house the knights of the langue of Castile, Leon, and Portugal. The heraldic symbols of the grand master, the crescent moon, can be seen in the omega-hood mouldings above the windows.

Entrusted with this project was the Maltese architect Andrea Belli, whose auberge reflects an era of growing national pride in a small European state under the sovereign rule of a wealthy, energetic prince. This highly decorative yet relatively restrained baroque edifice continues to delight the viewer through its grandiose design, subtle details and balanced proportions. The ascent to the main door is made on an elegant podium of low-rising steps. Pinto's bronze bust is proudly displayed on the pediment above the entrance amidst a festoon of banners and war trophies. The arms of Castille and Leon can be seen above the cornice.

The favourable site occupied by the auberge was initially intended to house the Grand Master's Palace, but this plan was abandoned in 1571. Following French rule, the auberge was used as the headquarters of the British Army. Today it is the office of the prime minister.

St James Cavalier

Valletta's land front is dominated by two imposing cavaliers. These raised earth platforms built on the bastions were designed to mount artillery and to command the surrounding grounds. They are, in all respects, independent forts. Of the nine cavaliers proposed by Francesco Laparelli, only two were built. Flanking the city's main gate, these are St John and St James cavaliers.

The British used St James cavalier as barrack accommodation, storage of ammunition, a officer's mess, a water reservoir, as well as a food store known as the NAAFI. As Malta's Millennium project, St James was converted into a centre for creativity. The cavernous ascent which was once used as a ramp to transport cannon to the rooftop is now an elegantly lit staircase welcoming art enthusiasts to its sky-lit atrium, theatre, exhibition halls, cinema, gift shop, and café. This edifice is a fine example of innovative design with a deep respect for the past.

Reconstruction of St James cavalier, bastion, and counterguard.

Left: Art exhibition at St James Cavalier
Middle: The cavalier; a fort in its own right.
Right: Concert recital inside the music room.

Lascaris War Rooms

The Lascaris War Rooms are a complex of underground tunnels dug beneath Lascaris Bastion that were converted into control centres for the Allied Army, Air Force, and Navy during the last war. The meticulously preserved shelter complex is one of four remaining World War II Military Operations Rooms open for pubic in the world today. From here Allied commanders Dwight Eisenhower and Bernard Montgomery planned the invasion of Sicily (code named *Operation Husky*) that began on 9 July 1943. Inside the war rooms are dioramas of war scenarios complete with giant wall maps, three-dimensional models, and plot tables 'operated' by life-size mannequins that faithfully recreate the atmosphere of the Battle of Malta (1940-43).

Above: Reliving history inside the Lascaris War Rooms.
Below: The Garrison Chapel converted into the Malta Stock Exchange.
Bottom: The Garrison Chapel at night.

Garrison Chapel

In 1850 the Garrison Chapel-School was built to serve as a place of worship for the Protestant British garrison and as a school for young soldiers and their children.

The various British military regiments stationed in Malta commissioned paintings to embellish the chapel, mostly from the famed local artist, Giuseppe Cali (1846-1930) whose bust stands behind the chapel inside the Upper Barrakka Gardens. The commissions included a set of life-size paintings depicting Old Testament prophets and the apostles and are said to be among the artist's finest. Eleven of these paintings are to be found in the Russian chapel at San Anton Palace, Attard.

Following the closing of the chapel in 1950, it was reopened in 1953 as an entertainment hall for the Services with dances and film shows. Later, it was used as the Central Mail Room of the General Post Office until, in 2001, after two years of restoration, it reopened as The Malta Stock Exchange.

Opposite: The colourful Malta Buses.

Above: The serene atmosphere at the Upper Barrakka Gardens.

Upper Barrakka Gardens

The Upper Barrakka gardens are situated on St Peter and St Paul's bastion. Strolling along the paths of this historic garden, it is hard to imagine that this same garden was once used by the desperate French troops to grow crops when they were blockaded inside Valletta between 1798 and 1800. The Italian knights used this area as training grounds but, with the departure of the French in 1800, the garden was opened to the public. Since then the garden has played both a ceremonial and a recreational role.

Monuments have been erected here as a tribute to the achievements and hardships endured by the Maltese, to commemorate important local and foreign personalities, as well as to remember tragic incidents at sea. These include the bronze sculpture known as a copy of *Les Gavroches* by local sculptor Antonio Sciortino (1879-1947) (the original is in the Museum of Fine Arts) and the busts of Sir Winston Churchill and Maltese

Below: The garden retains its charm at night.

painter Giuseppe Cali. Between 1907 and 1973, two elevators, better known as the Barrakka Lifts, made a 52-metre ascent from Customs House below to provide access to Valletta.

The view from the belvedere is breathtaking. From left to right the harbour coast unfolds as follows: Valletta and Ricasoli breakwaters, Fort Ricasoli, Bighi Hospital, Kalkara Creek and the village of Kalkara, Fort St Angelo and the town of Vittoriosa, Dockyard Creek, Cospicua, Senglea, French Creek, Corradino Heights, and Marsa. A closer look will reveal the extensive Cottonera Lines running an impressive 4.5km enclosing the Three Cities of Vittoriosa (Birgu), Cospicua (Bormla), and Senglea (Isla). Beneath the gallery is a saluting battery that fires a shot everyday at noon.

Below: Saluting battery firing the cannon at noon.

Next Page:
Top: Notre Dame de Liesse church at the water's edge.
Bottom: Cornice above the doorway to the Auberge d'Italie – detail.

The Aqueduct
In its early days, Valletta lacked a reliable water supply and the city had to rely on water collected in wells and cisterns. Grand Master Alof de Wignacourt solved this problem by constructing an arched aqueduct that carried water some 9 km from the springs west of Mdina to Valletta. On 21 April 1615 water gushed out from the fountains of the capital amidst the rejoicing of the people. The aqueduct is still extant and can be seen in the towns of Hamrun and Fleur de Lys. One of the surviving Valletta fountains lies behind the Opera House ruins with the Latin inscription Omnibus Idem *which translates 'to everyone the same'.*

Notre Dame de Liesse Church

Notre Dame de Liesse church was built by architect Andrea Belli for the knights of the French langue in 1740 to replace one constructed in 1620 by Bailiff Giacomo Chenn de Bellay.

The church was damaged by enemy action during the war. Despite some later unfaithful restoration, the elegant features that enhance this tiny temple can still be appreciated. Worthy of mention are the graceful squat dome capped by a neat lantern and the belfry designed by Francesco Zammit.

Liesse church stands at the foot of Marina Hill, a thoroughfare that leads to Victoria Gate (formerly Del Monte Gate). Opposite the church once stood the old fish market and the famous Neptune statue that now graces the Palace courtyard.

In the past this area bustled with activity and Notre Dame church offered spiritual respite to the visitor entering or leaving the city. This road is still commonly referred to as Liesse Hill but today the church stares dismally at a traffic-island.

Auberge d'Italie

The Auberge D'Italie was designed in 1574 by Gerolamo Cassar as a one-storey building; in 1582 a second floor was added to accommodate the growing number of Italian knights. The head of the Italian langue was traditionally the admiral of the navy; a prestigious post within the hierarchy of the Order. Affixed to the walls of one of the rooms, a tablet records the great victory over the Turks at the Dardanelles in 1656. In the council chamber, a series of oil paintings illustrates the various phases of that battle. Above the entrance, Grand Master Gregorio Carafa's bronze bust is surrounded with all sorts of honorary motifs carved out of white marble. This marble is believed to have come from a large pillar that once stood in the Roman temple of Proserpine, not far from Mdina. Following the destruction of the Auberge d'Auvergne in 1942, the Auberge d'Italie served for a time as the seat of the law courts. The Auberge D'Italie houses the Malta Tourism Authority (MTA).

Castellania Palace

Situated at the corner of Merchant's Street with St John's Street is the Castellania Palace. The Castellania; the Civil and Criminal Tribunal of the Order, owes its name to the president of these tribunals known as the 'castellan'. The Castellan was appointed by the grand master from one of the seven langues of the Order (the English Langue being suppressed after Henry VIII's Reformation of 1534) and held office for a term of two years.

The first Castellan Palace was built during the reign of Grand Master la Cassière on the site of the present edifice. In 1757 work began on the new Castellania. For this project, Grand Master Pinto appointed the Maltese architect Francesco Zerafa (1679-1758) who died before seeing his palace completed by Giuseppe Bonnici (1707-79).

Above: Statue representing Justice inside the Castellania Palace.

The Castellania is one of the finest baroque palaces in Valletta. The portico, surmounted by a wrought iron balcony set amidst Corinthian pilasters is made out of rich Carrara marble. The highlight of the façade is set within the open-curtain motif contained by the cornice above the balcony. It consists of a dramatic sculptural arrangement of three allegorical female figures, namely, Glory, Justice and Truth. Glory is seen holding a trumpet, proclaiming the virtues of the grand master. Truth holds a mirror in her right hand and strangles a serpent with her left while Justice, clutching a sword in her right hand is missing a left hand which almost certainly held a pair of scales.

Below: Detail from Castellania façade showing allegories of Glory and Justice.

Here in 1905, the physician and archaeologist Sir Themistocles Zammit discovered the Mediterranean strain of brucellosis, commonly known as 'undulant fever'. He identified unpasteurized milk as the major source of the pathogen.

THE MALTA BUSES

The first buses that appeared in Malta were BMC Thornycroft types and operated from St Julian's to Valletta. They became instantly popular and the success of the bus forced the railway and the tramway services to close down. In 1932 buses were coloured according to their routes and in the late seventies they were all painted green. Nowadays the bright orange Malta buses and the grey-and-scarlet Gozo buses consist mainly of Leyland and Bedford Plaxton models. The interiors are typically decorated with saints' niches, painted slogans and a wealth of superstitious symbols. New models are replacing the old ones, which may be more comfortable but not as charming.

Below: Palazzo Parisio – for seven days headquarters to Napoleon Bonaparte.

Palazzo Parisio

At the top of Merchants Street, opposite the Auberge d'Italie, stands Palazzo Parisio. The palace was built on the site of two houses previously owned by the Ventimiglia family. Despite its sober appearance, the palace retains a simple elegant quality. The only noticeable features are the elaborate central doorway and the charming windows on the top floor.

The palace secured its fame when Napoleon Bonaparte took up his quarters here between 14 and 20 June 1798. En route to Egypt to sever he British trade routes to India, the Corsican general recognized Malta's value as a vital communication point for his campaign. On 9 June 1798, the *Orient* and a flotilla carrying over 49,600 troops appeared off the Maltese shores. Overwhelmed by such a force, Grand Master Hompesch's 600

knights, of whom 200 were French, had no choice but to hand over their island home.

In eventful six days, Napoleon promulgated the revolution's values of Liberty, Equality, and Fraternity. However, following months of anticlerical French regime and extensive plundering of the island's national treasures, the Maltese revolted and, aided by a British blockade at sea, expelled the French after a two-year siege.

On 26 November 1800, Sir Ralph Abercrombie, commander of the Egypt expedition, called at Malta and, like Napoleon before him, lodged at Palazzo Parisio. During World War II, the palace was damaged by enemy action. Since 1973 it has housed the Ministry of Foreign Affairs.

Above: General Napoleon Bonaparte
Below: St James – church of the Castilian knights and façade detail.

St James' Church

The church of the knights of Castille, Leon, and Portugal is the first example of an elliptical baroque interior in Valletta. The use of the ellipse by Romano Carapecchia was more the result of necessity rather than choice. The conflicting use of the circular plan with liturgical function (requiring the altar to be placed in the spiritual focus of the church) led architects to experiment with the elliptical form. The circular opening above the choir provides a source of light illuminating Filippo Paladini's titular painting of *St James*. The exterior, with its skilfully projected and recessed decorative elements, unfolds a delightful spectacle of light and shade. The meticulous detail gives St James' church an enduring sophisticated appearance.

MARSAMXETT HARBOUR

GREAT SIEGE ROAD

MARSAMXETT GATE

ST ANDREW'S BASTION

ST MICHAEL'S BASTION

ST ANDREW STREET

MARSAMXETT STREET

SAPPERS STREET

MATTIA PRETI SQUARE

WINDMILL STREET

M A VASSALLI STREET

ST PATRICK STREET

ST MARK STREET

17

19

OLD MINT STREET

ST JOHN BASTION

ST JOHN CAVALIER

CAVALIER STREET

SOUTH STREET

MELITA STREET

OLD BAKERY STREET

ST JOHN STREET

POPE PIUS V TREET

ORDNANCE STREET

STRAIT STREET

BUS TERMINUS

16

18

REPUBLIC STREET

CITY GATE

ZONE 2

Opposite: Old Mint Street and Carmelite Church dome.

Palazzo Ferreria

Palazzo Ferreria, sited on the old foundry of the knights, occupies an entire city-block and it was erected in 1875. It belonged to John Lewis Francia, a wealthy business entrepreneur whose activities included the running of the National Flour Mills, as well as a leading local banking firm.

Palazzo Ferreria is a blend of classical, Venetian, and Maltese architecture that is somehow both alien and familiar to the streets of Valletta. The Maltese limestone here lends itself to create foreign exotic motifs and the traditional wooden balcony is incorporated in the façade to complete the Melito-Venetian fusion.

During the *Sette Giugno* riots of 1919 (also known as the bread riots), the palace which symbolized bread production in Malta suffered destruction by the angry mob. Hitler's *Luftwaffe* further contributed to the devastation by blasting away the original balconies to pieces in 1942.

Top: The old foundry of the knights.
Above: Palazzo Ferreria in Republic Street.
Below: Hastings Garden with St John cavalier in background.

Hastings Garden

This garden is named after Lord Francis Rawdon (1754-1826), Marquis of Hastings. Hastings had fought in the War of American Independence and later, as governor-general of India, he strove to establish British sovereignty over the various military states of that country. In 1824, he was appointed governor of Malta, a position he held for less than three years.

Designed by A. Woodford in 1826, Hastings' monument takes the form of a neo-classical temple hosting the governor's sarcophagus. The garden spreads over two bastions, namely, St John and St Michael bastions and is connected by a rectangular walk. As a backdrop to the garden stands the imposing St John's cavalier, today the embassy of the Order of St John.

The elegant Msida Yacht Marina can be admired from the lower part of the garden, over St Michael bastion. The seaside town of Sliema and charming Ta' Xbiex with its cluster of embassies can also be enjoyed from here. Between Sliema and Ta' Xbiex, on an island rises the impressive stronghold known as Fort Manoel.

Ever since 1569, when work on Valletta's defences was still underway, serious concerns arose on the vulnerability of this section of the city's bastions that could be attacked from the little island across Marsamxett Harbour. In 1723 work began on a square-shaped fort financed by the popular Grand Master Anton Manoel de Vilhena on the little island which would bear his name.

Duelling
Duels were common sport during the time of the knights. According to the 18th century travel writer Patrick Brydone, in Valletta these took place in the narrow Strait Street where combatants settled their scores screened by the tall buildings, hidden from the eyes of the law. The penalties for duelling included imprisonment, expulsion from the Order, and even execution.

Auberge de Provence

The Auberge de Provence looms over the busiest commercial area in Republic Street. Built around 1575 to the design of Gerolamo Cassar, it was to experience various alterations. The present mannerist façade is generally attributed the French architect Mederico Blondel and dates to the late 17th century.

Below: Auberge de Provence, today the National Museum of Archaeology.

The majestic assembly hall on the first floor of the Auberge de Provence, with its ivory panelled walls richly decorated with flower, fruit, and bird motifs, is one of the finest rooms in Valletta. Here the knights indulged in sumptuous banquets prepared by expert French chefs. A number of dishes per course were placed on their tables and the brethren, served on silver plates, ate away as they fancied washing everything down with fine imported wines. A traveller who ate at the table of the Provencal knights once claimed that the game consumed there was 'fatter than anywhere in Europe'. The head of the langue of Provence was the grand commander and he presided over the Order's treasury.

From 1826 to 1955, the edifice served as the Malta Union Club, a prestigious club whose members included dignitaries like Benjamin Disraeli, Sir Walter Scott, and the Prince of

Wales (later King Edward VII of England). In January 1958, The Malta National Museum was inaugurated and the auberge housed both the Fine Arts and Archaeological collections. In 1974, the Fine Arts collection was moved to its present site in South Street and the museum was renamed The National Museum of Archaeology.

The National Museum of Archaeology

The Archaeological Museum is divided into six exhibition rooms, each containing samples and artefacts relating to a specific time phase in Neolithic Malta. These treasures bear testimony to an inspiring human achievement of universal significance. Collectively, five temples of the Maltese islands (mainly those of Skorba, Mnajdra, Ta' Ħaġrat, Ġgantija, and Ħaġar Qim) are listed on the prestigious World Heritage Site list. Together with the Ħal Saflieni Hypogeum and the walled city of Valletta, Malta has the largest density of World Heritage Sites per square kilometre.

Room 1 (photo b): These artefacts are from the Għar Dalam phase (5200 BC) down to the Żebbuġ phase (3800 BC). They include decorative clay animal heads, flint blades, and imported greenstone, probably used to make necklaces.

Room 2 (photo c): This room houses preliminary temple-building models as well as building tools and other objects unearthed on site. These include a floral altar, fragments of a temple façade model, and stone blocks decorated with pig, ram, and sheep reliefs.

Room 3 (photos d, i, k): The numerous statues and statuettes displayed in this area are shrouded in mystery. The identity of these corpulent asexual figurines is debatable but the little evidence available points towards a female deity. Enjoying the limelight in this room is the so-called *Venus of Malta*; a female palm-sized statuette of superb craftsmanship.

Opposite: Valletta door knockers.

Room 4 (photo e): This room showcases a handful of peculiar objects probably related to astrology. Most have lunar and solar markings as well as star-like incisions on them. It is widely accepted that the Maltese temples were built according to the movements of the skies. Also on display are clay amphorae from the middle of the temple period (*c.* 3500 BC).

Room 5 (photo f): This room is the sanctuary of the famous *Sleeping Lady*. Discovered at the Ħal Saflieni hypogeum, its level of craftsmanship rivals that of the *Venus*. The function of this portly female is cause for much debate.

Room 6 (photos a, g, h, j): The largest hall in the museum contains stone blocks and altars unearthed at the Tarxien temple. The evolution in decorative techniques is evident from the precise spiral patterns adorning the massive blocks. This precision, mastered through the use of primitive tools consisting of nothing more than sticks and stones, is a remarkable achievement of the ancient world.

The National Museum of Fine Arts

The edifice which houses the Museum of Fine Arts stands on one of the oldest sites that were built in Valletta. A striking feature in this 18th-century *palazzo* is its refined and elegant rococo staircase. Between 1821 and 1961, the palace served as the official residence of the commander-in-chief of the British fleet in the Mediterranean. In fact it is still referred to as Admiralty House.

The Fine Arts Museum was moved from the auberge de Provence to here in 1974. A respectable collection of 13th- to 20th-century paintings adorn its walls, many of which were funded by charitable individuals or institutions. Artists like Guido Reni, Louis Du Cros, Domenico Tiepolo, Giuseppe De Nittis, Hubert Robert, Girolamo Gianni, and Claude J. Vernet are represented here. The Mattia Preti collection and the works of local sculptors Melchiorre Gafà and Antonio Sciortino are not to be missed.

Above: The elegant staircase at the National Museum of Fine Arts.

The Visit by Antoine Favray (1706-98)

Favray's depictions of upper-class life in Malta are mostly treasured by the locals for their faithful reproductions of Maltese 18th-century costume. The artist makes good use of his brush in recreating fine silks and precious jewellery. At a time when this genre of portraiture was extremely rare, Favray excelled at giving the viewer a glimpse of aristocratic life inside opulent homes adorned with ornate furniture, lavish curtains, and exquisite paintings.

Judith and Holofernes by Moise Le Valentin (1591-1632)

In the wake of the fiery and ill-tempered Caravaggio, a handful of *caravaggisti* are identified with the choice of dramatic scenes from the Bible, an uncompromising sense of realism, and mastery of the light and darkness interplay known as *chiaroscuro*.

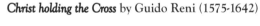

Christ holding the Cross by Guido Reni (1575-1642)

Like his master Annibale Caracci, the painter from Bologna is primarily concerned with 'beautifying' nature. Unlike Caravaggio's 'naturalist' approach with its faithful representation of 'nature as it is', the Caracci tradition seeks to return to the classical ideals of beauty in art. Christ's movements appear gentle and His posture loose. Only the way the lighting plays on His supple body marks a departure from Renaissance art.

The Valletta views by Louis Du Cros (1748-1810)

Vedute paintings found their niche in the 18th and 19th century. Just as Constable and Lorrain faithfully recreated scenes of English countryside and Canaletto and Guardi those of Venice, so can 18th century Valletta be brought to our eyes thanks to the brush of the Swiss painter Louis Du Cros.

The Martyrdom of St Catherine by Mattia Preti (1613-99)

The Martyrdom of St Catherine is a favoured theme with Mattia Preti. Despite comparisons with the Renaissance master Michelangelo, the Calabrian Preti has a very unique style. In this painting, the muscular executioner thrusts towards the delicate, luminous frame of the martyr creating a whirl of movement set in an architectural background beneath a stormy sky. The artist's choice of colours is warm and vibrant. This combination of ecstatic religious experience and vivid colour schemes made Preti a favourite with his patrons, the grand masters of Malta.

Antonio Sciortino (1879-1947)

After the prodigious Melchiorre Gafà (Bernini's pupil), Malta had to wait for well over 200 years to bring forward a sculptor of international acclaim. Sciortino was to carry the torch in this field of art. Exhibiting works at the Paris Salon and The Royal Academy in London brought the sculptor from the village of Zebbug worldwide approval and foreign commissions. His legacy is well documented in this museum.

'The fortifications of Valletta are endless. When I first walked about them, I was struck with their strangeness and when I came to understand a little of their purpose I was overwhelmed with wonder.'

Samuel Taylor Coleridge, 1806

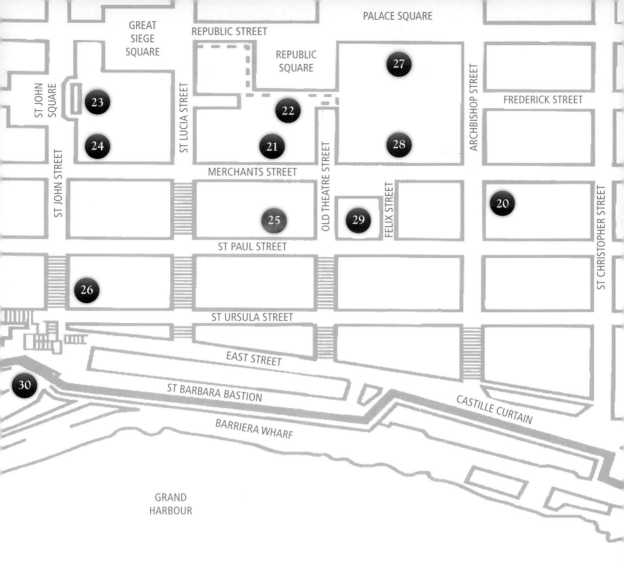

ZONE 3

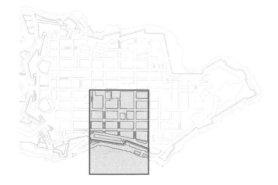

Opposite: Bridge over Old Theatre Street connecting the Grand Master's Palace with the National Library.

Jesuit Church, Oratory, and College

The Jesuit church and its former college complex comprises the entire block bordered by Merchants Street, Archbishop Street, St Paul Street, and St Christopher Street. The four corners of the edifice are graced by four statues of Jesuit saints, Ignatius of Loyola, Francis Borgia, Aloysius Gonzaga, and Francis Xavier.

Ignatius of Loyola (1491-1556), founder of the Jesuit movement had long wished to set up a college in Malta. In 1592, by authority of Pope Clement VIII and with the efforts of Grand Master Verdalle and Bishop Gargallo, a Jesuit College in Malta was founded. The Jesuits were pioneers of education in Malta. Prior to their arrival, anyone wishing to pursue higher learning had to go to Sicily. The new college conferred degrees in philosophy and theology.

The foundation stone of the Jesuit church and college, designed by Giuseppe Valeriano (1542-1596), was laid in the summer of 1595. In 1634, following an explosion of a gunpowder magazine that damaged the entire building, reconstruction was entrusted to Francesco Buonamici. The oratories of the Immaculate Conception and St Onorata within the complex are a dizzying spectacle of intricate lacelike stonework. Buonamici's remodelling of the church's façade and interior sparked off the genesis of baroque architecture in Gerolamo Cassar's mannerist city.

Above: Jesuit church façade.

Below:
Left: Main altar, Jesuit church.
Centre: Oratory of Saint Onorata.
Right: Oratory of the Immaculate Conception.

At 4 a.m. on 23 April 1768, the Jesuits were suddenly awakened and set on board a ship bound for Civitavecchia. Under diplomatic pressure from European sovereigns, Grand Master Pinto had been forced to expel the Jesuit community. The college became a university in 1769. In 1968, the University of Malta moved to its present site at Msida.

Municipal Palace

The Municipal Palace in Merchants Street was once the Valletta town hall. Its site was previously occupied by the Treasury of the Order which had a second entrance on what is today known as Old Treasury Street. Commissioned by Italian Grand Master Marc'Antonio Zondadari, the Municipal Palace was completed in 1721 to the design of Romano Carapecchia. It was the seat of the Valletta *Università* and the *Consolato del Mare*.

The Valletta *Università* was a form of town council responsible for ensuring fair trade as well as safeguarding the interests of the various guilds (such as goldsmiths, masons, and cobblers) that worked in the city and the harbour towns. This representative body was also entrusted with collecting the Order's taxes and with the maintenance and illumination of the streets of Valletta and the Three Cities. The *Consolato del Mare*, set up in 1697, was a maritime tribunal consisting of four (later six) consuls and dealt with all claims and counterclaims pertaining to shipping activities.

Grand Master Zondadari had declared Malta's harbour a 'free port' to all Christian shipping. His bust is set amidst an exquisite carved trophy above the central window. Carapecchia's Municipal Palace brought to Valletta a breath of baroque liberation that became the prevalent sentiment of the Order in the 18th century. The edifice is nowadays home to the Public Registry.

Saints and Sinners

As fighting monks, Hospitallers were bound with vows of purity and chastity. However, the hot blood of the warrior inside often led these monks astray. The Spanish Grand Master Nicolas Cotoner notoriously had a special taste for prostitutes. Grand Masters Perellos and Verdalle mysteriously contracted venereal disease, while the French Grand Master de Paule was in the company of his courtesan just before he died.

Below: The Municipal Palace, nowadays the Public Registry.

Enjoying a coffee in scenic Republic Square.

The Maltese *Gallarija*

The old wood-enclosed balcony or gallarija is a dominant feature of Maltese architecture. The first of these projecting glass and timber structures appeared in the Grand Master's Palace's corner of Republic Street with Old Theatre Street in the late 17th century. The gallarija became immensely popular and, soon enough, similar structures sprang up all over the capital's facades. These wooden extensions create an ideal space for hanging clothes to dry or for a prying housewife to spy on her neighbours undetected. During the village festa, the entire family crams into the gallarija to throw confetti on the holy statue and procession below.

The National Library

Before the arrival of the knights, Malta possessed only a handful of scattered libraries belonging to the religious orders. Their use was limited to a few scholars, namely priests and monks.

During the chapter general of 1555, the possibility of setting up a library was discussed but the ever-growing threat of a Turkish invasion and the siege of 1565 meant that the project was shelved for almost a century. During the magistracy of Lascaris (1636-57), the conventual church of St John was to spare one of its rooms to serve as a library. This library owed its existence to the collection of books left by the deceased members of the Order which, by statutory decree, automatically became property of the *Comun Tesoro*.

In 1760, Bali Fra Ludovico Guerin de Tencin came across a fine collection of books that was sent from Rome and that had belonged to the late Cardinal Gioacchino Portocarrero. De Tencin bought the cardinal's 9,000 volume collection and, together with his own personal literary miscellanea, donated everything to the Order to give birth to the island's first public library or *Bibliotheca Pubblica*. It was then just a large old house in Republic Street.

The library soon outgrew its premises. In 1776, Grand Master De Rohan chose the land between St John's church and his palace as the site for the new *Bibliotheca* which was designed by Stefano Ittar. This was to be the last public building erected by the knights in Malta. With the French troops occupying the islands in 1778, Ittar's dream library could have easily become De Tencin's nightmare. The French, ever intent on preying on Maltese heritage, were miraculously prevented from destroying the precious archives of the Order thanks to the efforts of one Gaetano Bruno and through the timely rebellion of the Maltese.

In 1812, during the governorship of Sir Hildebrand Oakes, the present *Bibliotheca* and its treasures were finally opened to the public. Its many riches include the original Bull of Pope Pascal II instituting the Order of the Hospitallers dated 1113; the Deed of Donation of the Maltese Islands and Tripoli to the Order by Charles V in 1530; and the correspondence that passed between the grand masters and sovereigns of Europe, such as Louis XIV, Henry VIII, and Empress Catherine of Russia. Other items of interest include a 1496 incunabulum describing the siege of Rhodes of 1480 and a precious 1426 illustrated manuscript depicting the life of St Anthony the Abbot.

Top: The Deed of Donation of the Maltese Islands to the Order of St John of Jerusalem by Emperor Charles V, 1530.
Above: The National Library, home to the archives of the Order of St John.

St John's Co-Cathedral

In 1573 Grand Master La Cassière commissioned Gerolamo Cassar to design the church of St John to serve as the new conventual church. It took five years to complete. The design allowed for side-chapels to occupy the space in between the buttresses that hold the structure in place. The rather unimpressive mannerist façade contrasts with its opulent baroque interior. The sumptuous heart of the church is the masterstroke of the Calabrian artist Mattia Preti who, between 1661 and 1666, transformed the austere interior into a showpiece of baroque magnificence. Successive grand masters and benefactors took great pride in embellishing it with the countless works of art. The result is a dazzling spectacle of colour, radiating luxury from every nook and cranny. The sacrilegious plunder of the finest gold and silver by Napoleon's troops between 1798 and 1800 did little to obscure the majesty of St John's church.

The Vault Paintings

As part of the redecoration of St John's, Mattia Preti painted the barrel-shaped vault of the temple with episodes from the life of the patron saint of the Order. He divided each of the six bays of the vault into three vignettes, resulting in an 18-episode narrative of the saint's life ending with his tragic beheading at the hands of Herod.

The splendid interior of St John's co-cathedral.

52

The Marble Tombstones

The floor of the entire temple is made up of some 375 polychromatic marble inlaid tombstones. Beneath them are buried high dignitaries of the Order, the flower of the nobility of Europe. These memorials bear Latin inscribed eulogies professing the qualities of the deceased and are adorned with the coat of arms of their noble occupants amidst grim symbols of death.

The Chapels of the Langues

On either side of the nave are the chapels of the various langues, dedicated to their respective saints. The conventual church united under one roof brave knights of different nationalities and national loyalties, competing to create the most lavish chapel of all. The chapel of Provence is dedicated to St Michael; Auvergne to St Sebastian; France to the Conversion of St Paul; Aragon to St George; Italy to St Catherine of Alexandria,; Castille to St James the Less; Germany to the Epiphany; and the Anglo-Bavaria to St Charles Borromeo. The chapels contain a wealth of artistic treasures such as the painting of Preti's *St George and the Dragon* in the chapel of Aragon and the beautiful silver gate in the chapel of the Blessed Sacrament.

The Grand Masters' Crypt

The crypt is the final resting place to 12 of the 28 grand masters to rule in Malta, namely, L'Isle Adam, del Ponte, d'Homedes, de la Sengle, del Monte, La Cassière, Verdalle, Alof de Wignacourt, Garzes, Vasconcellos, Ximenes, and de Valette. Their monuments are sculptural masterpieces worthy of princes. The ceiling of the crypt was decorated with frescoes by Nicolò Nasoni. After 1623, the deceased grand masters started being interred in ornate marble mausoleums above ground in the chapels of their respective langue. Their monuments sculpted with symbolic angels, slaves, and war trophies are masterpieces of baroque funerary art.

Top: Marble tombstone with high baroque ornamentation
Middle: The chapel of the langue of Italy.
Bottom: St George and the Dragon in the chapel of the Aragonese langue.

The Oratory

The Oratory houses two of the most valuable art treasures in Malta, *The Beheading of St John the Baptist* (1608) and *St Jerome Writing* (1607) by Michelangelo Merisi da Caravaggio. The *Beheading of St John* is Caravaggio's largest painting and his only signed work. The artist's name is inscribed in the martyr's blood as *F Michelan*. The brutality of the scene unfolds in all its drama through the stark contrasts of light and darkness and has earned this masterpiece the title of 'the painting of the 17th century'. The *St Jerome* depicts the frail saint in an austere setting exposed to a mystifying intense light that accentuates his tired old muscles. St Jerome is best known for his translation of the Bible from Greek into Latin. Underneath the Oratory is a second burial chamber known as the Crypt of Bartolott where members of the Order were buried.

St John's co-cathedral commissioned in 1573 by Grand Master La Cassière.

Great Siege Graveyard
The open ground flanking the co-cathedral on the Merchants Street side is known as the Campo Santo. Beneath the monument surmounted by a crucifix lie buried 256 knights who died heroically fighting during the siege of 1565. A plaque affixed to the side lists the names of the deceased brethren.

Museum of St John's Co-Cathedral

Flemish Tapestries: The most valued treasure in the museum is a set of 14 large and 14 smaller Flemish tapestries donated by Aragonese Grand Master Ramon Perellos in 1702. They were woven in Brussels on the looms of Judecos de Vos, court weaver to French King Louis XIV and are based on cartoons by Peter Paul Rubens (1557-1620) and Nicolas Poussin (1594-1665).

Illuminated Manuscripts: Another prized collection in the museum is that of the 17 choral books and 18 illuminated manuscripts dating back to 1533. They are the gifts of Grand Masters L'Isle Adam, Verdalle, and de Paule. These books are inscribed in fine Gothic script on parchment and are decorated in silver, gold, and coloured illumination.

Top: 'The painting of the 17th century' – Caravaggio's The Beheading of St John.
Middle and Bottom: Details from The Beheading of St John.

The museum also contains a wealth of paintings, sacred vestments, and precious altar accessories such the silver and bronze monstrance for the relic of St John. This monstrance contained a golden reliquary that originally housed the relic of St John the Baptist's forearm. The reliquary was stolen by Napoleon on his way to Egypt while the last grand master, Ferdinand Hompesch, took the precious relic with him in 1798, never to be seen again.

St Paul Shipwrecked Church

St Paul Shipwrecked church in St Paul's Street dates back to 1639. The architects who contributed to this building were Bartolomeo Garagona, the renowned Lorenzo Gafà, and Dr Nicola Zammit who designed the present façade. Over time, St Paul church amassed one of the largest silver treasures on the island. It also possesses the relics of the right arm of St Paul enshrined in a silver reliquary and part of the pillar on which the saint was beheaded. The titular statue of St Paul is the work of Melchiorre Gafà, a Maltese Rome-based sculptor whose talents had been recognized by the baroque master Gian Lorenzo Bernini.

On his way to Rome to be tried and executed, St Paul the Apostle was shipwrecked on these shores in AD 60 and resided here for three months. During his stay, he converted the local Roman Governor Publius to Christianity and appointed him the first bishop of Malta. The feast of St Paul's shipwreck, patron saint of the Maltese, is celebrated on 10 February.

Above: Statue of St Paul by Melchiorre Gafà
Far left: The silver reliquary holding the relic of St Paul's right arm.
Left: Part of the pillar on which St Paul was beheaded.

St Mary of Jesus Church (*Ta' Ġieżu*)

The Franciscan church of St Mary of Jesus at the lower end of St John's Street was one of the first churches in Valletta. The present façade dates back to the late 17th century and, like most of the early buildings erected in the city, it was designed by Gerolamo Cassar.

Inside, resting on the altar of the Crucified Jesus is the 'miraculous crucifix' made by the Fra Umile Pintorno in 1630. This crucifix, which is synonymous with this church, is a much treasured artefact and a focus of reverence to its many devotees. It is said that while the saintly Fra Umile was sculpting the figure of Christ, Jesus' head was found miraculously in its rightful place. Outside, on the St Ursula Street side of the church, is a delightful carved niche sculpted by Maestro Gianni. The stepped descent from St John's co-cathedral to the *Ta' Ġieżu* church down through Victoria Gate with Fort St Angelo in the distance makes this one of the most photographed paths in Valletta.

The Snow Depot
Climate was no obstacle for the knights of Malta. The demand for ice-cold lemonades and cool wines during the torrid summer months necessitated the regular shipment of ice from the snowy mountain caps of Sicily, some 95 km away. The ice was tightly packed in deep wells for better conservation and later sold by weight from a shop in St Ursula Street. In today's value, ice would cost about €4 per kilo.

Opposite: The city at work.
Below: The steps of St John's Street leading to the church of Ta' Ġieżu.

*Above: The Grand Master's Palace
Below: The statue of Neptune in the Prince
of Wales Courtyard.*

The Grand Master's Palace

The Grand Master's Palace was built close to the site where a Turkish battery had pounded St Elmo during the siege of 1565. It was originally intended to be built on the site now occupied by the Auberge de Castille but Grand Master del Monte favoured this stretch of land in the heart of the city. In 1571 the council of the Order bought the house belonging to his nephew, Eustachio del Monte, with the aim of building the Magisterial Palace on this site. Del Monte died the next year and his successor Grand Master La Cassière completed the project. Gerolamo Cassar's design incorporated the previously built barrack within the new structure. Evidence of this hindrance is in the unsymmetrical windows in the lower floor. In 1741 Grand Master Pinto tried to restore some harmony in the architecture of the palace. A second monumental portal was opened in the façade and another wooden balcony wrapped around the Archbishop Street side of the structure. The two portals give access to the two courtyards now known as the Prince of Wales Courtyard and the Prince Alfred Courtyard respectively. The former is characterized by the imposing bronze statue of Neptune, God of the Seas (supposedly modelled on Admiral Andrea Doria) while the latter is graced above by the Pinto Turret Clock. The halls at the rear of the palace which house the Palace Armoury Museum were once used as stables. The grand master could avail himself of palace workforce totalling 150 men, including bakers, guards, coachmen, book-keepers, drummers, and 12 young pages.

Kukkanja
In 18th-century Valletta, Carnival cele-brations reached a climax with the popular Coccagna (Kukkanja) in Palace Square. The Coccagna consisted of a lattice of ropes held firmly by a high and thick pole decked with all sorts of exquisite foodstuffs. The poorer classes flocked into the square to try their luck at snatching the elusive prizes and perhaps reach the top of the structure for the grand cash prize. The grand master concluded the event by throwing coins to the populace.

Below: Graphic reconstruction of the Grand Master's Palace.

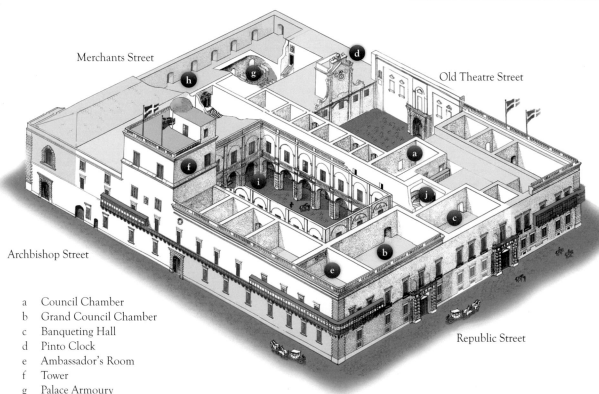

Merchants Street

Old Theatre Street

Archbishop Street

Republic Street

a Council Chamber
b Grand Council Chamber
c Banqueting Hall
d Pinto Clock
e Ambassador's Room
f Tower
g Palace Armoury
h House of Representatives
i Neptune's Statue
j Grand Staircase

61

The Council Chamber

The walls of this noble hall are hung with ten priceless Gobelin Tapestries donated by Spanish Grand Master Ramon Perellos in 1710. They depict exotic scenes of life in the jungles of India, Africa, and South America and were purchased from the renowned Parisian looms of Louis XIV. Below the ceiling are 14 frieze paintings illustrating 17th-century naval battles of the Order. The knights assembled in here to discuss affairs of state. Following the grant of partial autonomy under the British in 1921, the hall was home to the Maltese parliament until 1975 when this was transferred to its present location above the Armoury Hall.

The Grand Council Chamber

The Grand Council Chamber or Throne Room is decorated with a set of 12 mannerist frieze paintings representing key moments during the siege of 1565. They were painted in 1576 by Matteo Perez d'Aleccio who had worked with Michelangelo on the Sistine Chapel. The walls of the hall are covered in gleaming yellow damask. At the end of the hall, below the Arms of the Republic of Malta stands the chair of state, used by the president of Malta. Opposite the chair of state hangs the minstrel's gallery which was once part of the grand carrack Sant'Anna which brought Grand Master L'Isle Adam and his knights to Malta on 26 October 1530. During official functions the grand master sat on his throne below the gallery beneath a crimson velvet canopy with gold fringes.

The Banqueting Hall

Also known as the State Dining Room, this hall was badly damaged during World War II but has been restored to its former splendour. The walls are embellished with portraits of British sovereigns and Maltese presidents while the ceiling is crossed with timber rafters with gilt pendants in between.

Opposite:
Left: Parliament entrance.
Middle: Palace balcony on Old Theatre Street.
Right: Detail from Great Siege fresco in the Grand Council Chamber.

The Pinto Clock

Towering above the Prince Alfred Courtyard is the famous Pinto Clock, made by local artisan Gaetano Vella in 1745. It is surmounted by four bronze figures of Turkish slaves wielding hammers, striking the hours on a gong. The clock's four dials tell the time, day, month, and the phases of the moon. In 1894 the clock was silenced during the night-time hours by Governor Sir Arthur Fremantle to allow him to sleep undisturbed.

The Ambassador's Room

This is where foreign envoys presented their credentials to the grand master. In keeping with tradition, the president of Malta today still receives ambassadors in this hall. The walls are covered in red damask while a 16th-century Bohemian crystal chandelier hangs from the ceiling. The paintings below the ceiling represent episodes from the early days of the Order in Cyprus and in Rhodes.

The Tower

The Palace Tower rises above Neptune's Courtyard on the Archbishop Street's side of the edifice. It was probably built during the magistracy of Verdalle and served as a mint and treasure deposit of the Order. At five storeys, it was the highest structure in Valletta and offered unobstructed views of vessels entering and exiting the two harbours. In 1783 Grand Master de Rohan set up a stellar observatory on top of the tower equipped with the best astronomical instruments of its time.

The Palace Armoury

By the late 12th century, the knights of St John had grown considerably. Manning 27 strongholds across the Middle East, principally with mercenaries and native forces, was no small feat. Unconventional at the time, the Order took a large share of liability in arming and equipping its mercenary and native forces.

The origin of a centrally-governed armoury is traceable to the Order's early days in Outremer and Rhodes. The size of this array of arms and armour can only be speculated upon since no precise records have been found.

After the fall of Rhodes in 1522, the Order's armoury was inevitably exhausted. Grand Master Philippe Villiers de L'Isle Adam's desperate prayers for assistance from European monarchs did not go unnoticed. In 1531, a vessel laden with 20,000 crowns' worth of weapons arrived in Malta. It was a gift from King Henry VIII of England and it formed the backbone of the new armoury. When Grand Master Aloph de Wignacourt ordered the transfer of the armoury inside the palace walls in 1604, the significance of the collection grew as a showpiece of military power.

Under French and British rule, the armoury suffered looting and selected pieces were shipped to England. The true extent of this pillaging may never be known. Despite this abuse, the armoury still stands as an impressive original assemblage of armaments serving men of honour who have valiantly fought at the farthest outposts of the Christian faith.

Top: Turkish Sipahi arms and armour c. 1565.
Middle: Knights' cuirassier harnesses (Italian 17th century).
Left: A knight in half-armour during the time of the Great Siege.

Right:
a: Morion (Italian c.1560).
b: Falling-buffe (Italian c.1580).
c: Breastplate (Italian c.1550).
d: Buckler (Italian c.1580).
e: Dagger with scabbard (North African c.18th century).

Below: Turkish Sipahis during the time of the Great Siege.

Valletta Market

The area presently occupied by the Valletta Market building has a long history of commercial activity generated by a daily outdoor market. As early as 1640 this area, formerly an open square, used to accommodate a large number of makeshift stalls that sold agricultural produce and livestock.

The present building was designed by Hector Zimelli in 1859. It was inspired by Baltard and Callet's Les Halles market building in Paris (now demolished). The interior space of the market reveals the exposed metalwork that suspends the roofing structure. A raised skylight showers the stalls with natural light.

The market's architectural elegance may be at times contrasted by the occasional vociferous dispute, the random rattle of crates, and the customary ear-splitting claim of exceptional quality produce.

Top: Butcher at the Valletta Market.
Above: Interior of the market.

Open Market

A section of Merchants Street near the Valletta Market attracts locals and tourists daily to the Valletta Open Market. On Sundays, a flea market takes place outside the city walls beneath St James bastion, a stone's throw away from the bus terminus. Malta lace, traditional foodstuffs, cheap clothes, sea-shells, housewares, CDs, DVDs, antiques, and a fine selection of books are among the items to haggle over while taking in the frenzied atmosphere.

Victoria Gate

Victoria Gate, on the Grand Harbour side of Valletta, is a dual-carriage gate flanked by two pedestrian entrances and surmounted by the British Royal Arms. Designed by Emmanuele Luigi Galizia (1830-1906), it was inaugurated in 1885, in the 48th year of reign of Queen Victoria after whom it takes its name. The present gate replaced the Del Monte Gate. This gate was one of the three principal entrances originally designed for the city; the others being Porta San Giorgio (today's City Gate) and Marsamxett Gate on the opposite side of Valletta.

The old Del Monte Gate, a single-entrance gate with a drawbridge, was built by Francesco Laparelli for Grand Master del Monte in 1569. During the knights' and British eras, this area became a hive of activity and the gate provided access to the city from the bustling quay below. The steps at the rear of the gate lead to St John's Street and to the heart of Valletta. To the left of the gate was once an enclosed lush garden known as *Gnien is-Sultan* (The Grand Master's Garden) where grandasters could stroll amidst trees and flowers enjoying the views of the Grand Harbour. The garden no longer exists but a charming wall fountain survives behind the incongruous block of flats and the elegant cupola of Liesse church.

Above: From the harbour, Victoria Gate offers the shortest route into the heart of the city.

Above and below: Carnival floats parade towards Valletta.
Left and opposite bottom: Dressed to impress
in colourful costumes.
Right: Carnival scene, Palace Square c.1900.

CARNIVAL

Carnival Sunday occurs seven weeks before Easter. The origins of the Maltese carnival can be traced to the early 15th century but the festival's popularity soared thanks to the religious Order of St John. During carnival, the knights held plays in their auberges, filled the streets with streamers, and drank and revelled in the celebrations wearing hideous and hilarious masks. The nobility threw a grand ball inside the Manoel Theatre while, in the squares outside, music accompanied the processions and staged combats. Today, carnival kicks off with the parata; an old sword dance originated by the knights to commemorate the victory of the Great Siege. Vibrantly coloured floats parade through the streets, while the masses gather in Freedom Square to enjoy a dance, song, and drama spectacle.

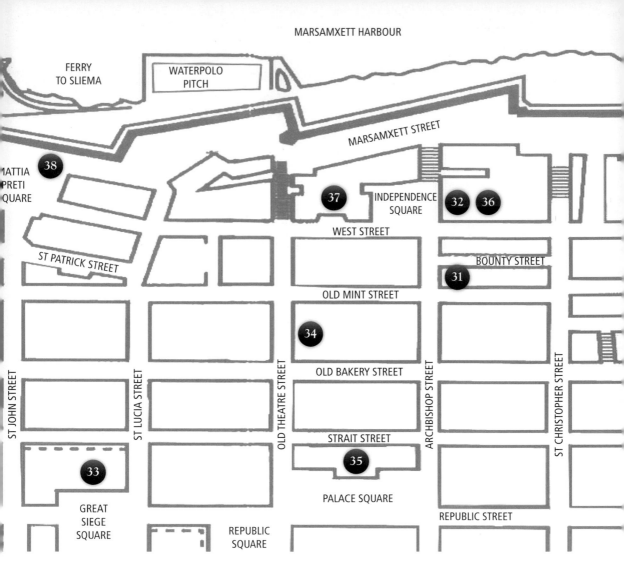

MARSAMXETT HARBOUR

FERRY
TO SLIEMA

WATERPOLO
PITCH

MARSAMXETT STREET

MATTIA
PRETI
SQUARE

38

37

INDEPENDENCE
SQUARE

32 **36**

WEST STREET

ST PATRICK STREET

BOUNTY STREET

31

OLD MINT STREET

34

OLD BAKERY STREET

ST JOHN STREET

ST LUCIA STREET

OLD THEATRE STREET

ARCHBISHOP STREET

ST CHRISTOPHER STREET

STRAIT STREET

35

33

PALACE SQUARE

GREAT
SIEGE
SQUARE

REPUBLIC
SQUARE

REPUBLIC STREET

ZONE 4

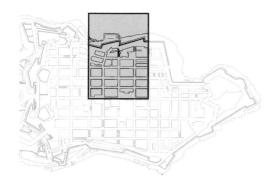

31 Archbishop Palace
32 Auberge d'Aragon
33 Law Courts
34 Manoel Theatre
35 Main Guard
36 Our Lady of Pilar Church
37 St Paul's Anglican Pro-Cathedral
38 The *Manderaggio* (demolished)

Left: Aerial view of Valletta with its parallel streets leading to Fort St Elmo.

Archbishop Palace

The rather unimpressive Archbishop's Palace is situated close to the Auberge d'Aragon just off Independence Square is the creation of Maltese architect Tommaso Dingli who also designed of the old Valletta gate which is now replaced by an unfitting gaping hole, quite alien to the noble city of the knights.

During construction, the palace was caught in the constant heated debate between grand master and bishop. Grand Master Alof de Wignacourt, preoccupied with the bishop's presence a stone's throw away from his own palace, went so far as to obtain a temporary inhibition from Pope Urban VIII on the grounds that the new bishop's residence was intended to interfere with the Order's jurisdiction within the new city. Bishop Cagliares claimed that his powers legitimately extended over the whole island and that this inhibition was utterly discriminating.

Above: The Old Mint Street corner of the Archbishop's Palace.
Below: Auberge d'Aragon with the monument to the heroes of the failed 1799 conspiracy opposite.

Construction of the palace soon resumed on the site formerly occupied by a fresh water spring that had apparently dried up. This spring, however, still delivers fresh water under the palace to this day. The Archbishop's Palace boasts a splendid sunken garden; a rarity for this gardenless city.

Auberge d'Aragon

The Auberge d'Aragon, Catalonia, and Navarre on Independence Square opposite St Paul's Anglican pro cathedral is the auberge still most faithful to Gerolamo Cassar's original design. A rather sombre one-storey building, it reflects the earlier architectural disposition of the knights in Malta. The original Auberge de Castile must have looked something like this before it was rebuilt in the baroque style in the 18th century. Completed in 1572, the Auberge d'Aragon had several spacious halls surrounding a central courtyard. The Aragonese was the grand conservator responsible for the supplies of the Order.

Between 1921 and 1972, the Auberge d'Aragon served as the office of the prime minister. Nowadays it houses the ministry for justice and home affairs.

Law Courts

The law courts in Republic Street stand opposite the Great Siege monument commemorating the victory over the Turks in 1565. The three bronze figures represent Civilization, Malta, and Religion respectively. The neo-classical courthouse with its monumental Ionic portico was completed in 1971. It stands on the site of the auberge of Auvergne, whose head was the grand marshal and the supreme commander of all the armed forces of the Order. During the British period, the auberge served as a courthouse until it was devastated by a German parachute mine in 1942. Nowadays, the massive colonnade of the law courts lends shade to a gathering of argumentative, laid-back pensioners.

1799 Conspiracy

After just three months of repressive Napoleonic rule, Maltese rebels pushed the French garrison to retreat behind the walls of Valletta. Under the leadership of a brave clergyman, Don Michele Mikiel Xerri, a plan was hatched to overthrow the besieged garrison from inside the city during the early hours of 12 January 1799. The plan was uncovered and 50 conspirators were arrested. Five days later Don Michele and his group were shot by a French firing squad in Palace Square. A monument to the heroism of Fr Xerri and his men stands in front of the Auberge d'Aragon in Independence Square.

Below: The law courts in Great Siege Square.

Manoel Theatre

The magistracy of the Portuguese Grand Master Manoel de Vilhena (1722-36) brought a period of modernization and prosperity in Malta. The fears of a Turkish threat abating, the knights and the Maltese could devote more time to the pursuit of pleasure.

Vilhena commissioned this theatre, then called *Teatro Pubblico*, in 1731. Before that day, comedic or musical performances were held at the *Corpo di Guardia* (today's Main Guard opposite the Palace) or in the auberge of Italy (Merchants Street).

The *Teatro Pubblico* was designed by the Italian Romano Carapecchia (1668-1738). Like so many other buildings in Valletta, its austere façade belies its rich interior. It seats 650 and its acoustics are second to none. The hushed turnings of an orchestra conductor can be heard clearly throughout the auditorium.

The theatre was inaugurated on 19 January 1732 with the acclaimed tragedy by Scipione Maffei, *La Merope*. It is reputed to be the third-oldest working theatre in Europe. Part of the inscription above the theatre's entrance reads '*ad honestam populi oblectionem*' summing up the grand master's philosophy behind its construction: 'for the honest recreation of the people'. For over half-a-century, this theatre served as the 'coliseum' of the Maltese and their overlords in the new city.

The French and the British also made ample use of the theatre. Renamed the *Teatro Reale* in the early 19th century, the auditorium would host a regular solid crowd of British officers in search of amusement. The glory days of Vilhena's *Teatro* were eclipsed in 1866 when the new Theatre Royal (Royal Opera House) was inaugurated.

Opposite: The splendid rococo interior of the Manoel Theatre.
Top: A former bar in Strait Street.
Middle: Old stage costumes in the Theatre Museum.
Bottom: The auditorium (detail).

Strait Street
During British occupation, the narrow Strait Street thronged with sailors in search of alcohol, fistfights, and ladies of the night. 'The Gut', as it came to be known throughout the Empire, was lined with bars and music halls such as Union Jack and Blue Peter. Today only the graffiti on the walls survive to tell the seedy tale.

Top: The Main Guard's portico in Palace Square.
Above: The de Rohan fountain on the Archbishop Street side of the Main Guard.

Mattia Preti's House
The Italian master painter responsible for decorating the interior of St John's Cathedral resided on a modest, two-storey 16th-century house in Marsamxett Road overlooking the harbour. The house still stands today and it is located a few steps away from the foot of the spire of St Paul's Anglican Cathedral.

As a consequence, the old theatre became a lodging house for beggars and between the two wars it also served as a cinema. Restoration works began in 1956 and the Manoel, as it came to be affectionately called, soon regained its former dignity as the heart of social interaction.

Main Guard

Opposite the Grand Master's Palace, across Palace Square, stands the building today known as the Main Guard. During Valletta's early years, this one-storey edifice was the armoury of the Order and housed all the arms and armour of the knights. It was then called the *Armeria Pubblica* (Public Armoury).

In 1604 Grand Master Wignacourt ordered that the *Armeria Pubblica* to be transferred within the Magisterial Palace; a plaque on the Main Guard's façade commemorates this event.

The Greek Doric portico was added in 1814. It is the work of Maltese architect Giorgio Pullicino. At the time, the classical style was being favoured by the British as a symbol of imperial propaganda. The projecting doorway supports the armorial shield of Great Britain and the Latin inscription reads: 'To great and unconquered Britain, the love of the Maltese and the voice of Europe confirms these islands. AD 1814.'

The two fountains flanking the Main Guard were constructed during the reign of Grand Master de Rohan. Water sprouts from the mouth of a triton surmounted by an imperial eagle.

Opposite page:
Top: The church of the Aragonese knights in West Street.
Middle: Ornate door knocker (Our Lady of Pilar church).
Bottom: St Paul's Anglican pro-cathedral opposite the Auberge d'Aragon.

Our Lady of Pilar Church

The church the Virgin of Pilar was the house of worship of the Aragonese knights. It is located right behind the Auberge d'Aragon and it is dedicated to the apparition of the Virgin Mary to St James the Greater in AD 40. Tradition holds that while St James was preaching the gospel in Spain, Our Lady appeared to him and gave him a small wooden statue of Herself and a column of jasper wood and instructed him to build a church in her honour.

The present Pilar church was designed in 1718 by Romano Carapecchia to replace an earlier church severely damaged during the earthquake of 1693. The interior is one of the most elaborate compared to the churches of the various langues. Sculpted angels with gilt wings hover around the walls of the temple and wrap around the columns behind the main altar. The altarpiece by local artist Stefano Erardi shows *The Apparition of Our Lady to St James*. Recently the church has undergone restoration works. It has been officially handed over to Heritage Malta with the aim of being re-opened to the public.

St Paul's Anglican Pro-Cathedral

In the early years of British occupation, the Maltese ecclesiastical authorities feared the possibility that the foreign rulers would attempt to convert the island populace to Protestantism. Knowing all too well how sensitive the Maltese were regarding religious matters, the British overlords tried to appease the local Roman Catholic authorities as much as possible.

That was until the Dowager Queen Adelaide's arrival in Malta in 1838. She personally financed the construction of an Anglican church to cater for the spiritual needs of the British troops and Protestant residents in Malta. The site chosen was that occupied by the German auberge which was still partially intact when the foundation stone of St Paul's was laid on 20 May 1839.

The project was entrusted to Richard Lankesheer who, although succeeded in designing the elegant neo-classical temple, proved incompetent in understanding the properties of the local stone. Half-way through construction, cracks and splits were already visible and three Maltese workmen lost their lives when parts of the building collapsed in September 1842.

Director of Engineering Works to the Admiralty William Scamp replaced Lankesheer following the latter's death (presumed suicide) in 1841. Scamp was in Malta working on the Number One Dock in Cospicua and later on the Naval Bakery in Vittoriosa.

St Paul's Anglican cathedral was inaugurated by the bishop of Gibraltar on All Saints Day 1844. Together with the Carmelite church dome, the-90 meter bell-tower of St Paul's dominates the Valletta skyline.

The *Manderaggio*

Descending behind St Paul's Anglican pro-cathedral, the residential quarter bordering Mattia Preti Square right above Marsamxett Gate is known as the *Manderaggio*. The name *Manderaggio* or *Mandraki* refers to the inner part of a harbour or haven. Laparelli's original designs for Valletta included an inland dock on this side of the harbour that could hold up to ten galleys. The quarried stone from the site was to be utilized for building purposes. This project was later abandoned as the quality of the stone proved inadequate. Over the years, slum housing filled in this 'quarry' and the area with its closely packed houses and poor sanitary facilities became synonymous with poverty, disease, and crime. After World War II, the entire quarter was replaced by blocks of flats. To this day, for many Maltese the word *manderaggio* still carries negative connotations.

Opposite: Valletta street niches.
Top and middle: Interior of St Paul's Anglican pro-cathedral.
Bottom: The narrow streets of the old Manderaggio quarter.

Next page: Dome and crowning statue (St Dominic church).

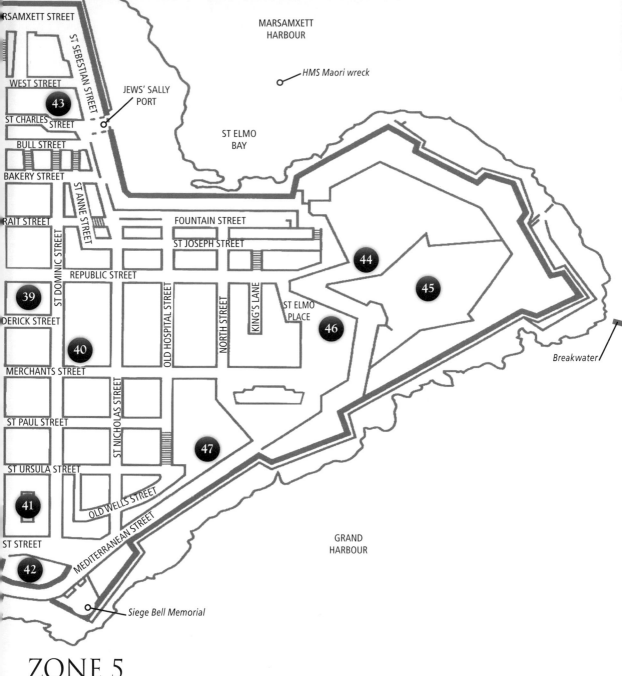

MARSAMXETT
HARBOUR

RSAMXETT STREET

ST SEBESTIAN STREET

WEST STREET

43

JEWS' SALLY
PORT

ST CHARLES STREET

BULL STREET

BAKERY STREET

ST ANNE STREET

RAIT STREET

ST DOMINIC STREET

REPUBLIC STREET

39

DERICK STREET

40

MERCHANTS STREET

ST NICHOLAS STREET

ST PAUL STREET

ST URSULA STREET

41

OLD WELLS STREET

ST STREET

MEDITERRANEAN STREET

42

Siege Bell Memorial

FOUNTAIN STREET

ST JOSEPH STREET

OLD HOSPITAL STREET

NORTH STREET

KING'S LANE

ST ELMO
PLACE

46

47

ST ELMO
BAY

HMS Maori wreck

44

45

Breakwater

GRAND
HARBOUR

ZONE 5

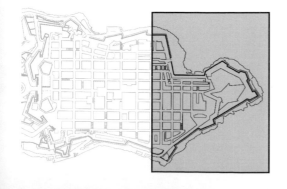

Casa Rocca Piccola

Built around 1580, Casa Rocca Piccola is named after its first proprietor Frà Pietro la Rocca, a distinguished Italian knight, admiral of the Order of St John, resident ambassador in Rome, and later envoy to the pope and the duke of Savoy.

On his death, Casa Rocca passed into the hands of the Italian knights until 1784 when it was sold to a Maltese nobleman and has been resided by Maltese families ever since. The present charismatic incumbent, the 9th Marquis de Piro, has generously opened up his doors for all to witness this unique *palazzo* that has changed little in over 400 years.

Its priceless treasures and collectables include antique Majolica pots, Bohemian chandeliers, 18th century silver surgical instruments, old documents, and fine paintings. Of particular interest are:

Above: Coat of arms of the de Piro family.
Below: The portable chapel and the Lascaris panels inside the library.

Opposite:
Top: The green room.
Middle: The golden sedan chair.
Bottom: The rock-hewn bomb shelter.

The Golden Sedan Chair: Donated by Grand Master Pinto to Frà Victor Nicolas de Vachon Belmont, the captain general of the galleys. Seated comfortably inside the plush interior of the sedan chair, Belmont would have been carried by four servants or slaves through the streets of Valletta, through corridors and upstairs.

The Portable Chapel: Inside the library is this black lacquered cabinet decorated with floral motifs that opens up into a chapel in its own right. The chapel includes valuable items such as silver statuettes, a crucifix, reliquaries, and chalices while the altar frontal opens to reveal a sacristy.

The Lascaris Panels: Another coveted part of the collection hangs above the library door. It is a set of five panels painted around 1640. These romantic representations of naval scenes once decorated the *Gran Salone* on board Grand Master Lascaris' ship. Their survival to this day has ensured them national patrimony status.

Costumes and Collections: The fifteen costumes together with many other related accessories such as spectacles, snuff-boxes and silver card-cases make up the Casa Rocca Piccola costume collection. Some of the costumes date back to the early 18th century and they offer a glimpse into past Maltese life.

Bomb Shelters: This *palazzo* also houses two wartime shelters. One is a well that during World War II could accommodate as many as 150 people and also function as a church on Sundays. The second shelter was a private one that was to serve the resident family and their servants.

Casa Rocca Piccola is a charming aristocratic house with a remarkable family history spanning over two centuries. Its rooms unfold a story of Maltese lineage enriched with the lives of painters, barons, generals, bishops, grandmasters, cardinals and popes.

Top: The winter dining room.
Above: The summer dining room.
Below: St Dominic church, dome.

St Dominic Church
(Our Lady of Fair Havens)

In 1569 Grand Master del Monte donated the land to the Dominican friars to build a small church dedicated to Our Lady of Fair Havens to cater for the spiritual needs of the first residents in Valletta. In 1571, Pope Pius V, benefactor of the city of Valletta, elevated the church to parish status. Today this status is shared with the church of St Paul Shipwrecked in St Paul's Street and St Augustine church in Old Bakery Street and is the cause of much rivalry among their parishioners. The feast of St Dominic is celebrated on the last Sunday of August. The present church was completed in 1815 to the design of Antonio Cachia. His originality lay in the concave treatment of the central segment of the façade. The ceiling of the church was embellished by the prolific Maltese painter Giuseppe Cali and his son Ramiro.

The Old Slaves' Prison

The 'Slaves' Prison' or *Gran Prigione* in Valletta was located opposite the Lower Barrakka, behind the Holy Infirmary. A large, three-storey edifice almost the size of the Grand Master's Palace, it was built during the rule of Grand Master Verdalle by Gerolamo Cassar.

The prison was administered by the *Prodomo* who had absolute power over the inmates. The prisoners consisted mainly of Muslim captives and local criminals. They were forced to work on the Order's galleys and in the various industries such as sail-making and in the bakeries. Slaves were also employed in households but had to return to their cells at night. The slave population in the early 18th century stood at around 6,000, with 1,000 of them being detained in the Valletta prison. The conditions in the *Gran Prigione* were deplorable. The cells were overcrowded and damp, the food disgusting, and the water stagnant. Rebellious behaviour by the inmates was suppressed with torture, beating, and execution.

Above: The staircase of the old slaves' prison. Below: The Lower Barrakka Gardens and the Siege Bell Memorial.

Nothing survives of the prison of the knights in Valletta. During the last war, a school that stood in its place was destroyed by German air attacks and in 1948 it was replaced by a huge and unsightly apartment block.

Lower Barrakka Gardens

The Lower Barrakka, situated at the lower end of Valletta forming part of St Christopher bastion overlooking the entrance to the Grand Harbour, offers a splendid view of the surrounding shoreline. Here rises the neo-classical monument to Sir Alexander Ball (1757-1809). Under Lord Nelson, Ball commanded the naval blockade against Napoleon's troops and led the Maltese insurgents against their French invaders during the siege of 1798-1800. He became the first British commissioner of Malta when the islands were annexed to Great Britain. His monument bears an inscription recording the esteem in which

the Maltese held this distinguished naval officer. Behind Ball's monument, through the arcades, one can see the Siege Bell Monument and World War II Memorial. They commemorate the 50th anniversary of the presentation of the George Cross to the Maltese Islands and honour the victims of the conflict. At 11 tons, the Siege Bell is the heaviest and largest bell in Malta. The bell tolls daily at noon.

Auberge d'Angleterre et de Bavière

The auberge of the Anglo-Bavarian knights was the only inn of residence not built for this purpose in the city. The military-styled building originally belonged to the bailiff of Acre, Frà Gasparo Carneiro. It was designed in 1696 by Carlo Gimach and named after its proprietor, Palazzo Carneiro.

When in 1540 King Henry VII estranged England from the Catholic Church in Rome, he confiscated the properties of the English knights and the langue of the Order ceased to exist. Some knights continued to serve in exile, but their numbers were too few to form a proper division. In 1784, during the reign of Grand Master de Rohan and with the consent of King George III of England, the amalgamated langue of Anglo-Bavaria was created, which, also united to the priory of Poland, acquired this building as its auberge. Like the English knights before it, the head of the new langue became turcopilier and commanded the Order's cavalry. He was also responsible for guarding the coasts from Ottoman attack.

Opposite: Archbishop Street steps descending upon East Street.

Top: Sir Alexander Ball's monument inside the Lower Barrakka Gardens.
Above: The auberge of the Anglo-Bavarian langue.

During British rule, the Auberge d'Angleterre and de Bavière was used as an army officer's mess and later as an elementary school. Despite suffering damage during the Second World War, the palace survives in its original state. Today it is home to the Government Property Division.

1675 Plague
On 4 December 1675, a young girl from Valletta was reported as suffering from a terrible fever and of bearing a number of red patches and pustules. She died within seven days: the first victim of a plague outbreak which, in less than a year, claimed the lives of 20% of the entire population. Valletta alone lost 4,000 of its 10,000 inhabitants. Many fled to the villages, while those who stayed behind were confined to their households, praying and making vows to the saint protectors of the plague, St Roche and St Sebastian. Grand Master Nicolas Cotoner regularly visited the stricken towns to console the locals and improve morale. The island was declared free from the plague in September 1676. The church dedicated to St Roche is in lower St Ursula Street.

The National War Museum

The National War Museum is situated at the lower end of Fort St Elmo in what was previously a powder magazine. This part of the historic fort was converted into a museum in 1975. The exhibits bear witness to the hardships endured by the Maltese between 1940 and 1943 when the dark cloud of World War II cast its shadows on the tiny island.

During the war Malta was a base for British submarines and aircraft preying on Axis supply lines trying to reach North Africa. Wave after wave of Italian *Regia Aeronautica* and German *Luftwaffe* air raids tried to bomb the island fortress into submission. In March and April 1942 alone, more bombs were dropped on Malta than fell on London during the entire blitz. Many architectural treasures were lost in these annihilation raids: the Royal Opera House, the auberges of France and Auvergne, and the Chapel of Bones to name a few. Axis aircraft routinely decimated relief convoys and the Maltese had to spend long stretches in crude underground shelters, subject to damp, disease, and hunger.

Above: The Malta George Cross.
Below: The devastated Royal Army Ordnance clothing store.
Bottom: The Gloster Gladiator 'Faith' on display at the War Museum.

On 15 April 1942, King George VI awarded Malta the George Cross with the words: 'To honour her brave people I award the George Cross to the Island Fortress of Malta, to bear witness to a heroism and a devotion that will long be famous in history.'

The George Cross is on display inside the museum, as is an Illuminated Scroll presented by President Franklin D. Roosevelt to the 'People and Defenders of Malta' on his visit here in 1943. An Italian E Boat, a section of a Spitfire, and a Gloster Gladiator are among the principal exhibits of the museum.

HMS *Maori*
Early morning on 12 February 1942 the British Tribal Class Destroyer HMS Maori berthed in Grand Harbour received a direct hit from an enemy plane and sank. Part of the wreck was later floated and moved to the bay just below Fort St Elmo some 100 metres opposite the Auberge de Bavière at a depth of 13 metres. The Maori is very popular with divers looking for an historic yet relaxed dive.

Fort St Elmo

Before the arrival of the knights, the tip of this promontory jutting out between the anchorages of Marsamxett and the Grand Harbour stood a small watch-post and chapel dedicated to St Elmo, patron saint of seamen. The tower guarded the entrance to the harbours. The constant threat of a Turkish raid emphasized the importance of building a better fortress on this strategic site.

The foundation stone of Fort St Elmo was laid in 1552 during the reign of Grand Master Juan d'Homedes. Architect Pietro Prado designed a star-shaped fort surrounded by a dry ditch. At the time, Valletta did not yet exist and the landward side of the fort was overlooked by the high grounds of Mount Sciberras.

During the Great Siege, the Turks mounted 24 pieces of heavy artillery on these elevated grounds and on 24 May 1565, the walls of St Elmo got their first taste of Muslim fury. The 900-man garrison of St Elmo faced an overwhelming force of 30,000 of Suleiman the Magnificent's troops well-equipped for siege

Top: Fort St Elmo defending the entrance to the harbours.
Middle: St Anne's Chapel, Fort St Elmo.
Bottom: Historical re-enactment inside the fort.

warfare. Against impossible odds, the brave knights and men held out for a month until, on 23 June, Turkish flags were seen fluttering on what remained of battered St Elmo. The last Christian defenders were mercilessly decapitated, nailed to wooden crosses, and sent floating across the harbour waters to Birgu where their comrades picked them up. The knights lost 1,500 men to the Turks' 8,000. The invaders suffered heavier casualties until their humiliating return to Constantinople at the end of the siege.

After the siege, St Elmo was rebuilt and in 1600 a beacon tower was erected on its walls to guide ships into harbour. In 1687 a series of enveloping walls known as Caraffa bastions, were constructed incorporating the bulwark within the architectural fabric of Valletta.

The second Great Siege came from the skies. On 11 June 1940, an Italian aerial attack on St Elmo left four gunners dead. They were the first Maltese victims of the Second World War. The historic fort nowadays houses the Police Academy and the War Museum. For many, St Elmo will always be remembered as the backdrop for the movie *Midnight Express*.

Above: The insurmountable walls of Fort St Elmo.
Below: Reconstruction of the fort c.1700.

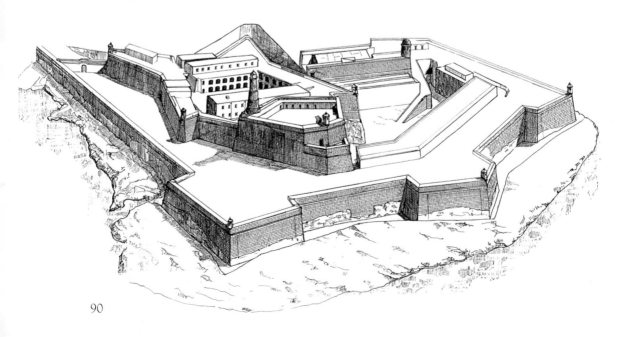

The Granaries

In the open grounds between City Gate and St Publius' church, as well as on the esplanade in front of Fort St Elmo, one will notice, protruding above the ground surface, a large number of round stone caps. These are the lids of the granaries of the knights, most of them during the rule of Grand Master Martin de Redin. The stone caps cover a complex of bell-shaped underground silos. Each cover is sealed with cement and rendered air tight. Grain thus stored lasts for years. The silos are very deep and each can contain up to 40 quarters (approx. 11,640 litres) of grain. These granaries were mainly intended to serve for the storage of wheat against times of war or emergency. The granaries were also situated in the area bordered by the Auberge de Castille and the Garrison Chapel. During World War II they stored precious food supplies that the convoys miraculously squeezed through the Axis blockade.

Chapel of Bones
In a parking area just opposite the Old Hospital of the knights, a signpost marks the spot where a famous chapel once stood. The Chapel of Bones was so called because its interior was decorated with hundreds of bones excavated by a local priest from a nearby cemetery. This once popular tourist attraction was destroyed during the last war.

The Holy Infirmary

For over 200 years, the walls of the Holy Infirmary, or *Sacra Infermeria*, enshrined the *raison d'être* of the Hospitallers in Malta. Before this nursing brotherhood developed into a military organization, the Order was solely concerned with nursing and protecting the sick and injured Christian pilgrims in the Holy Land.

The infirmary of the knights was the first international hospital organization in history for the welfare and service of the poor and the sick. Five hundred years after its birth in Jerusalem, the Order still prided in its hospitalling mission.

In 1574, Grand Master La Cassière commissioned Gerolamo Cassar to build an *ad hoc* hospital inside the walls of the new city. To accommodate the ever-growing number of patients, other architects later added new wards and rooms which make up the present vast complex.

Middle: The stone caps sealing the granaries.
Right: A Hospitaller knight caring for the injured in battle.

The Long Ward alone measures an impressive 155 by 10.5 metres. The infirmary had 900 individual beds' a rarity considering that most European hospitals catered for three or four patients per bed. Responsible for the hospital's administration were the French knights under their pilier, the grand hospitaller.

At the *Sacra Infermeria*, no discrimination was tolerated on religious or political grounds. Both Maltese and foreigners, irrespective of social status, were received here. Patients were treated to a diet of meat, bread, poultry, eggs, raisins, prunes, wine, milk, and vermicelli soup, all served on locally manufactured silver tableware. The wards were perfumed with rosemary and the walls were decorated with tapestries and paintings.

In 1676, a school of anatomy and surgery was founded here. Back then, surgeons and physicians already operated on the removal of cataracts and bladder stones. The *Sacra Infermeria* continued to fulfil its purpose under the French and British. In 1979, the building was converted into a first-class conference centre and Malta was awarded the *Europa Nostra Award* for its superb restoration.

Unwanted Babies

A room at the rear of the Sacra Infermeria catered for abandoned children. From the street outside, a mother could simply place the unwanted baby through a window inside a cot connected to a wheel. When the wheel was turned, the child found itself inside the room where it would be cared for by the hospital staff. The woman would therefore remain anonymous.

Right: La Valette Hall, formerly the Great Magazine Ward.

The Valletta Waterfront (Pinto Wharf)

This imposing array of warehouses stands outside the fortified walls of Valletta. These palatial-proportioned stores known as the 'Pinto stores' where built in 1752 at the expense of Grand Master Pinto. Mercantile shipping in Valletta burgeoned during the 18th century and the city's waterline bustled with the frantic loading and unloading of goods required at the tables of the knights and the courts of Europe. Malta's harbour was a free port to all Christian shipping and the marina became a vast clearing-house between east and west.

The cavernous vaults of the 19 warehouses once stored cargoes from the Levant and North Africa. Today they welcome tourists and locals to their sensibly converted interiors. Bars, restaurants, cafés, and souvenir shops line the shore of this historic harbour beneath the bastions of Valletta's suburb of Floriana. An elegant chapel designed by Andrea Belli, dedicated to The Flight of the Holy Family to Egypt, is tucked in between the warehouses facing the fortifications of Vittoriosa and Senglea.

Below: The splendid row of converted warehouses that make up the Valletta Waterfront.
Opposite: The fortifications of Valletta.

'That fair Valletta, with its streets of palaces, its picturesque
forts and magnificent churches... one of the most beautiful (cities),
for its architecture and the splendour of its streets...
something between Venice and Cadiz.'

Benjamin Disraeli, Firts Earl of Beaconsfield (1830)

ARTISTS' BIOGRAPHIES

Filippo Paladini (1544-1615)

The Italian mannerist painter Filippo Paladini was born in Casi, at Val di Sieve (Florence). In his early years, he worked in Vinci and Florence. In 1586 he was condemned to three years on the galleys for armed assault. When he came to Malta as a prisoner in 1588, his artistic abilities won him favour with the Order. During his stay here until his official pardon in 1595, he was kept busy with many painting commissions. For the knights of Castille, he painted the titular canvas of St James the Apostle for their church in Merchant's Street. He also decorated the grand master's chapel at the Palace with four frescoes depicting the life of St John the Baptist. The Jesuits' church also boasts a Paladini altarpiece, *The Circumcision of Our Lord Jesus Christ*. In Paladini's work we discover a sense of tense controlled emotion blended with a naturalist quality. The artist spent his last days in the Sicilian town of Mazzarino where he died.

Matteo Perez D'Aleccio (1547-1616)

Matteo Perez was born in Alezio, a small town close to Gallipoli in southern Italy. A disciple of Michelangelo Buonarroti, he worked on the Sistine Chapel and in Naples before his arrival in Malta in 1576. His early influence was that of the Venetian painters and his paintings with their elongated forms, unbalanced poses, manipulated irrational space, and unnatural lighting are characteristically mannerist. Among his greatest works in Valletta, D'Aleccio painted the original titular painting of St John's *The Baptism of Christ,* now preserved in the Co-Cathedral Museum. For St Paul's Shipwrecked church, he painted the altarpiece depicting the shipwreck of the Saint who is seen flicking the viper into the fire. His greatest achievement is the decoration of the Throne Room in the Grand Master's Palace with a set of 12 frescoes depicting the Great Siege of 1565 commissioned by Grand Master La Cassière. After leaving Malta, D'Aleccio travelled to Rome (Italy), Seville (Spain), and Lima (Peru) where he died.

Mattia Preti (1613-99)

Mattia Preti was born in Taverna, Calabria. He first trained in Naples under Giovanni Battista Caracciolo. Preti came into contact with the knights of Malta through Grand Master De Redin where in 1659 his skills as an artist brought him the prestigious commission of painting and decorating the conventual church of St John. Preti turned the austere-looking temple into the artistic treasure we see today. He decorated the vault with 18 paintings depicting episodes from the life of St John the Baptist. His *St George on Horseback* for the Aragonese chapel is a true masterpiece. For the church of St Catherine of Italy he painted *The Martyrdom of St Catherine*, which became a favourite theme with the artist. Preti lived and worked in Valletta for the last 40 years of his life. Nicknamed *il cavaliere calabrese*, he pioneered baroque art in Malta. Preti died at the age of 86 years and was interred in St John's.

Michelangelo Merisi da Caravaggio (1571-1610)

Michelangelo was born in Caravaggio, near Milan. At the age of 21, he went to Rome and soon forged important friendships in the capital of European art and established himself as master of *chiaroscuro* technique and venerated as an exceptional imitator of nature. His fame in art was shadowed by his criminal reputation. In 1606 he killed Ranuccio Tommasoni and fled to Naples to escape arrest. A year later, he arrived in Malta on board a galley of the Order of St John. Under Grand Master Alof de Wignacourt, he painted the *St Jerome Writing*, now in St John's, and the most famous *The Beheading of St John* in the Oratory of the same church. The latter painting is his only signed work and his name is written in the blood of the dying saint. Other works painted in Malta include the portrait of Grand Master Wignacourt, presently at the Louvre, Paris. Wignacourt was most impressed with the artist and on 14 July 1608 Caravaggio was received into the Order as a knight of obedience. A month later, he was involved in a brawl in Valletta and was imprisoned in Fort St Angelo. In October of that year, he escaped, and he was disgracefully expelled from the Order *in absentia*. He is the most important artist to set foot in Malta.

ARCHITECTS' BIOGRAPHIES

Francesco Laparelli (1521-70)

Francesco Laparelli, a soldier and a military expert, was born in Cortona, Italy. In Rome, he carried out defence works for Pope Pius IV on Castel Sant'Angelo together with Michelangelo Buonarroti. He was sent to Malta in late December 1566 by Pope Pius V. After the siege, the island's strongholds lay in rubble and Laparelli opted to build the new proposed fortress city of Valletta rather than restore the old forts to pristine condition. Laparelli wasted no time and quickly drew up plans for the new city with a land front at 500 canes from the walls of St Elmo. His proposals included the street grid-plan which facilitated artillery movement during sieges, a peripheral road that ran along the line of fortifications, as well as a galley pen and arsenal on the Marsamxett Harbour side (these last two plans never materialized). Laparelli opted for a dry ditch that cut across the land front from one harbour to the other with the cavaliers of St James and St John towering above. Before he left Malta in 1569, he entrusted the remaining works to Gerolamo Cassar. Laparelli died of the plague the following year in Crete.

Gerolamo Cassar (1520-1592)

The exact dates of birth and death of Gerolamo Cassar are not known. The Maltese born soldier, architect, and engineer is credited with the greatest architectural legacy in Valletta. As a soldier, he distinguished himself during the Great Siege. As an architect, he trained under Laparelli during the early stages of the city's construction. Following Laparelli's departure from Malta in 1569, Cassar took over as the Order's chief military engineer. He designed and supervised the building of St John's, the seven auberges of the langues (three of which were demolished), the Grand Master's Palace, the windmills and the bakeries of the Order (demolished), the Holy Infirmary, the Slaves' Prison (demolished), as well as a number of churches and private residences in Valletta. His mannerist style is characteristic of the knights' early military and humble disposition on the island. He is buried in the parish church of Our Lady of Fair Havens in Valletta.

Francesco Buonamici (1596-1677)

Francesco Buonamici was born to a noble family in Lucca, Italy. He arrived in Malta in 1636 as an assistant to Pietro Paolo Floriani, then working on the Floriana fortifications which defended the landward side of Valletta. For the next 20 years, he served as resident engineer and architect to the Order until his return to Lucca in 1659. In Valletta, Buonamici designed the church of St Nicholas and remodelled the Jesuit church in Merchants Street. The flamboyant Hostel Verdelin close to the Grand Master's Palace is also by him. He is responsible for introducing the classical, somewhat restrained, baroque style in Malta that would long dominate the architectural sphere of the island of the knights.

Romano Fortunato Carapecchia (1666-1738)

Carapecchia was born in Rome. At a young age, he was already a member of the renowned Accademia di San Luca (Rome) as a pupil of Carlo Fontana. Carapecchia arrived in Malta in 1707 during the magistracy of Perellos. He was primarily a water-supply engineer, but his Valletta buildings stand testimony to an architect with great versatility and creative drive. He designed the church of the Aragonese knights dedicated to Our Lady of Pilar and that of St Barbara belonging to the knights of Provence. He redesigned the elegant portico of St Catherine of Italy to which langue he belonged as servant-at-arms. In Merchants Street he built the grand Municipal Palace and St James church for the Castilian knights. The Manoel Theatre is perhaps his *magnum opus*. Carapecchia died of heart failure on 21 January 1738. He is buried in the Bartolott crypt in St John's co-cathedral.

Andrea Belli (1703-72)

Andrea Belli was born in Valletta on 13 October 1703. In his youth he lived in Rome with his family and later travelled to Germany and Austria from where, it is believed, he acquired his vividly ornate style. The magnificent Auberge de Castile is possibly his greatest architectural achievement. Attributions to Belli rest principally on stylistic grounds owing to a shortage of documentary evidence. It is safe to assume that the church of Our Lady of Liesse, the Museum of Fine Arts, the church of the Flight of the Holy Family to Egypt (at the Valletta Waterfront), and Palazzo Bonici (adjacent to the Manoel Theatre) are his. His unique style is characterized by meticulous detail combined with a flair for lush, yet elegant, ornamentation. Belli died on 19 October 1772 and was buried in the Carmelite church, Valletta.

APPENDIX

Grand Master of the Order of St John in Malta

Philippe Villiers de L'Isle Adam	1530 - 1534
Pierino del Ponte	1534 - 1535
Didier de Saint Jaille	1535 - 1536
Juan d'Homedes	1536 - 1553
Claude de la Sengle	1553 - 1557
Jean Parisot de Valette	1557 - 1568
Pietro del Monte	1568 - 1572
(moves convent to Valletta)	
Jean l'Evêque de la Cassière	1572 - 1581
Hughes Loubenx de Verdalle	1581 - 1595
Martino Garzes	1595 - 1601
Alof de Wignacourt	1601 - 1622
Luis Mendez de Vasconcellos	1622 - 1623
Antoine de Paule	1623 - 1636
Jean Paul Lascaris Castellar	1636 - 1657
Martin de Redin	1657 - 1660
Annet Clermont de Chattes Gessan	1660
Rafael Cotoner	1660 - 1663
Nicolas Cotoner	1663 - 1680
Gregorio Carafa	1680 - 1690
Adrien de Wignacourt	1690 - 1697
Ramon Perellos y Roccaful	1697 - 1720
Marc'Antonio Zondadari	1720 - 1722
Antonio Manoel de Vilhena	1722 - 1736
Ramon Despuig	1736 - 1741
Manoel Pinto de Fonseca	1741 - 1773
Francisco Ximenes de Texada	1773 - 1775
Emmanuel de Rohan Polduc	1775 - 1797
Ferdinand von Hompesch	1797 - 1798

British Civil Commissioners

Captain Alexander Ball	1799 - 1801
Major-General Henry Pigot	1801
Sir Charles Cameron	1801 - 1802
Rear-Admiral Sir Alexander Ball	1802 - 1809
Lieutenant-General Sir Hildebrand Oakes	1810 - 1813

British Governors

Lieutenant-General Sir Thomas Maitland	1813 - 1824
General the Marquess of Hastings	1824 - 1826
Major-General Sir Frederick Ponsonby	1827 - 1836
Lieutenant-General Sir Henry Bouverie	1836 - 1843
Lieutenant-General Sir Patrick Stuart	1843 - 1847
The Right Honourable Richard More O'Ferrall	1847 - 1851
Major-General Sir William Reid	1851 - 1858
Lieutenant-General Sir John Gaspard le Marchant	1858 - 1864
Lieutenant-General Sir Henry Storks	1864 - 1867
General Sir Patrick Grant	1867 - 1872
General Sir Charles Straubenzee	1872 - 1878
General Sir Arthur Borton	1878 - 1884
General Sir Lintorn Simmons	1884 - 1888
Lieutenant-General Sir Henry Torrens	1888 - 1890
Lieutenant-General Sir Henry Smyth	1890 - 1893
General Sir Arthur Freemantle	1893 - 1899
Lieutenant-General Lord Grenfell	1899 - 1903
General Sir Charles Mansfield Clarke	1903 - 1907
Lieutenant-General Sir Henry Grant	1907 - 1909
General Sir Leslie Rundle	1909 - 1915
Field-Marshal Lord Methuen	1915 - 1919
Field-Marshal Viscount Plumer	1919 - 1924
General Sir Walter Congreve	1924 - 1927
General Sir John Du Cane	1927 - 1931
General Sir David Campbell	1931 - 1936
General Sir Charles Bonham-Carter	1936 - 1940
Lieutenant-General Sir William Dobbie	1940 - 1942
Field-Marshal Viscount Gort	1943 - 1944
Lieutenant-General Sir Edmond Schreiber	1944 - 1946
Sir Francis Douglas	1946 - 1949

Sir Gerald Creasy	1949 - 1954
Major-General Sir Robert Laycock	1954 - 1959
Admiral Sir Guy Grantham	1959 - 1962
Sir Maurice Dorman	1962 - 1964

Governors General

| Sir Maurice Dorman | 1964 - 1971 |
| Sir Anthony Mamo | 1971 - 1974 |

Prime Ministers of Malta

Mr Joseph Howard	1921 - 1923
Dr Francesco Buhagiar	1923 - 1924
Sir Ugo Mifsud	1924 - 1927
Sir Gerald Strickland	1927 - 1932
Sir Ugo Mifsud	1932 - 1933
Dr Paul Boffa	1947 - 1950
Dr Enrico Mizzi	1950
Dr Giorgio Borg Olivier	1950 - 1955
Mr Dominic Mintoff	1955 - 1958
Dr Giorgio Borg Olivier	1962 - 1971
Mr Dominic Mintoff	1971 - 1984
Dr Carmelo Mifsud Bonnici	1984 - 1987
Dr Eddie Fenech Adami	1987 - 1996
Dr Alfred Sant	1996 - 1998
Dr Eddie Fenech Adami	1998 - 2004
Dr Lawrence Gonzi	2004 -

Presidents of Malta

Sir Anthony Mamo	1974 - 1976
Dr Anton Buttigieg	1976 - 1981
Ms Agatha Barbara	1982 - 1986
Mr Paul Xuereb (Acting President)	1987 - 1989
Dr Vincent Tabone	1989 - 1994
Dr Ugo Mifsud Bonnici	1994 - 1999
Professor Guido de Marco	1999 - 2004
Dr Eddie Fenech Adami	2004 -

BIBLIOGRAPHY

All places of publication are Malta, except where otherwise stated.

Abela, A.E., *Governors of Malta* (1991).

Attard, Joseph, *The Knights of Malta* (1992).

Bianchi, Petra and Peter Serracino Inglott, *Encounters with Malta* (2000).

Boffa, Charles. J., *Malta's Grand Harbour and its Environs in War and Peace* (2000).

Boffa, Charles J., *The Saga of the French Occupation, 1798-1800* (1998).

Bonello, Giovanni. *Art in Malta, Discoveries and Recoveries* (1999).

Bonello, Giovanni, *Histories of Malta. Vol. 1 Deceptions and Perceptions* (2000).

Bonello, Giovanni, *Histories of Malta. Vol. 2 Figments and Fragments* (2001).

Bonello, Giovanni, *Histories of Malta. Vol. 3 Versions and Diversions* (2002).

Bonello, Giovanni, *Histories of Malta. Vol. 4 Convictions and Conjectures* (2003).

Bonello, Giovanni, *Histories of Malta Vol. 5. Reflections and Rejections* (2004).

Bonnici, Joseph and Michael Cassar, *A Chronicle of Twentieth Century Malta* (2004).

Bonnici, Joseph and Michael Cassar, *Malta & Gozo, Then and Now* (1998).

Bonnici, Joseph and Michael Cassar, *The Malta Buses* (1989).

Bonnici, Joseph and Michael Cassar, *The Royal Opera House, Malta* (1990).

Borg, Joseph, *The Public Gardens and Groves of the Maltese Islands* (2005).

Borg, Malcolm, *British Colonial Architecture, Malta 1800-1900* (2001).

Cassar, Carmel, *A Concise History of Malta* (2002)

Cutajar, Dominic, *History and Works of Art of St John's Church Valletta* (1999).

De Giorgio, Roger, *A City by an Order* (1985).

De Lucca, Dennis, *Francesco Buonamici* (2006).

De Piro, Nicholas, *Valletta A City Built by Gentleman for Gentleman* (1997).